ADAMSON

RED RUMBA

RED RUMBA

A Journey through
the Caribbean and Central America

NICHOLAS WOLLASTON

READERS UNION

HODDER & STOUGHTON

London 1964

This RU edition was produced in 1964 for sale to
its members only by Readers Union Ltd at Aldine
House, 10-13 Bedford Street, London W.C.2 and at
Letchworth Garden City, Herts. Full details of
membership may be obtained from our London
address. The book has been reset in 10 point
Linotype Juliana leaded and printed by The
Northumberland Press, Gateshead on Tyne. It was
first published by Hodder & Stoughton Ltd.

Yo del inglés conozco pocas cosas,
Pués solamente hablo en español.
Pero entiendo a los pueblos cuando dicen,
'*Yankee, go home!*'

El inglés que yo tengo es muy escaso.
Es un inglés de '*Mister!*' y '*Hello!*'
Pero entiendo a los pueblos cuando exigen,
'*Yankee, go home!*'

Lo dicen en Manila y en Korea,
En Panamá, en Turquía y en Japón.
El clamor es el mismo en todas partes,
'*Yankee, go home!*'

Con este inglés me basta, aunque precario,
Para gritar con fuerza y con razón,
Y con criterio revolucionario,
'*Yankee, go home!*'

Me basta con mi voz nacionalista,
Para exigir con firma decisión,
Y con razones anti-imperialistas,
'*Yankee, go home!*'

Preface

THIS IS THE RECORD OF A JOURNEY MADE BETWEEN
February and June 1961. During those five months I went to ten
different countries, none of which I had ever visited before. Origin-
ally I had intended to go only to Cuba, but in the end curiosity—
about the other nine countries in general and about the effect of
the Cuban revolution on them in particular—led me from Cuba
through a circle of its Central American and Caribbean neighbours
and back again to Cuba.

Because it was the most important of them, I spent almost half
the time in Cuba, which meant that I was in some of the others for
only a week or two. But I make no apology to those people, whether
nationals or foreign residents of long standing, who may indig-
nantly cry, ' Well, what do you expect? He was only in the country
a few days.' Had I been a Spanish priest in Cuba, or a German coffee-
planter in Guatemala, or an Irish missionary in Haiti, or an American marine in Puerto Rico, let alone a subject of any of the ten
countries, I should doubtless have had very different things to say.
As it is, I was an English traveller, ignorant but interested, sometimes horrified, often confused, and always on the move; once or
twice, I admit, I was angry.

However, for his own purposes an inquisitive traveller soon learns
whose opinions are worth counting, and many of these I have
quoted; I have also quoted some whose opinions were certainly to
be discounted. I talked to communists and capitalists, to ambassa-
dors and peasants, to soldiers, doctors, shop-keepers, drunkards,
priests, prostitutes and Presidents. What they told me has prompted
much of what I have written. For the rest—my own observations—I
have no need of excuses.

Contents

List of Illustrations

between pages 96 and 97

11

COSTA RICA

Post Office

The Switzerland of Central America

PANAMA

Desolation

Rum and washing

HAITI

The capital

Soap-seller

The market

The Citadel

DOMINICAN REPUBLIC

The streets are clean

After Mass

PUERTO RICO

La Perla

Toyshop

I

Cuba: Havana

'NIGHT CLUB FOR SALE.'

It might have been a startling notice on a door in any other capital of the world, but in Havana in February 1961 it was no more extraordinary than the banners on the fronts of all the buses, 'Patria o Muerte!' It was a city of slogans, where the last feeble whispers of a once brash, but now expiring capitalism were drowned by the battle-cries of a victorious Fidelism. 'Death to the invader! We will conquer!' screamed the posters. 'We support nationalization!' shouted the plate-glass windows of a huge department store. 'Down with the assassins of Lumumba!' demanded the bullet-pocked façade of an old office building. In that building, two years earlier, a posse of Batista's officers had holed up on the top floor and been besieged; seven bodies had been brought down.

I went into the Floridita bar, where Hemingway used to sit beneath his own bronze bust, and asked for a daiquiri. I didn't know what to expect, and when it came, a champagne glass full of snow, I didn't know how to tackle it. I looked along the bar where a row of men were drinking Scotch, each with a bottle in front of him, and rolling dice. Two tarts, so outrageous that they were funny, were sitting together; their lipstick seemed to have been put on with a palette knife, smeared between chin and nostrils, and their skirts, zipped up under terrific pressure, were not quite tight enough to restrain their bottoms from oozing over the edge of the bar stools.

Two negroes with guitars came in, and one of them touched me on the shoulder.

'Cuban music,' he said. 'Real Cuban music.'

I turned back to my daiquiri, and sucked in a mouthful of snow

13

soaked in rum and lime juice and maraschino. It was neither a drink nor a water-ice, but delicious. A drunk started shouting across the room, and the silent little man next to me with his own bottle of Johnnie Walker on the bar looked round and slobbered dreamily; he was drunk too. In the entrance to the restaurant at the back of the bar, where empty tables were laid with clean linen and polished cutlery, the head waiter stood grinning. He wasn't angry, or even sad; he just wore an 'I-told-you-so' smile, and fiddled with a napkin. The tourists hadn't come for two years now. And Hemingway would never come again.

Outside, in the window of the sports shop next door, the dust was settling on the big game fishermen's spinning-rods and tackle. A grey-haired woman sat on a chair between the marble pillars of a bank, a rifle across her knees, and in the doorway of a cable office was a young girl in the uniform of a *miliciana*, with a Sten gun and a calm but anxious look in her eyes. A half-eaten orange flew past my face, flung from the window of a bus and followed by a jeer.

In the middle of the Parque Central a heap of red flowers lay at the foot of a plinth, with a purple ribbon tied to them. A label said, 'To the Apostle, from the ambassador of the Democratic Republic of Vietnam.' The man from Tonkin had arrived.

I looked up to see who the Apostle was, a white marble figure in nineteenth-century clothes with his hand stretched out as though he were feeding the swans. He was called José Martí. I had never heard of him before, but I had already noticed his portrait—tired eyes and long, melancholy moustaches—in several places. In Cuba, Martí's features are as common as quotations from his writings, and both are too common for the wants of an ordinary traveller.

I was hopelessly ignorant. I even thought that the slogan stretched across a shopping street, '*Paredón a los terroristas!*' meant 'Pardon for the terrorists!' and for half a day I credited the Cuban revolution with an unexpected quality of mercy. A week later I should never have made a mistake like that.

Through the saloon bar doors of Dirty Dick's throbbed the bass of a Wurlitzer juke-box; 'Late last night,' sang Bing Crosby, about ten years ago. Skippy's Hideaway was shut and padlocked. I went

14

into Sloppy Joe's—'first port of call-out, where the wet begins'—
and when I asked for a rum and ginger I was given a glass with a
lump of ice in it and two bottles, to help myself. Polished bar stools
stood like guardsmen against the bar, but nobody sat on them; I
was the only customer. Photographs of past patrons lined the walls
a little shamefully, the hang-overs of age-old revels; Frank Sinatra
was trapped in a laugh, the Duke of Windsor in a kindly, perplexed
smile. The notice above the bar, 'Alcoholic drinks are forbidden to
members of the armed forces of the revolution,' was signed by
Raul Castro.

'Do you want to go to the Tourist Institute, or do you want to
find out how we really live?' asked a Cuban businessman whom I
went to see next morning. 'Of course, there are no dead bodies in
the streets nowadays, and the police don't beat people up any more.
But business is very bad.' His fat eyelids almost burst behind his
dark glasses. His wife bustled about with drinks and family photographs in excruciating frames. On the door of their flat was a decla-
ration of faith: 'We are catholics, and we support the revolution.'
It was their insurance policy.

As the day got hotter, even though it was almost the coolest
time of the year, the streets began to smell of melting tarmac, and
the half-smoked cigar butts and discs of orange peel lying around
were slowly pressed by the traffic into the surface. Ice trucks on
their delivery rounds stopped to unload outside every other house,
and British buses burning Russian fuel filled the streets with hot
black fumes. In the Prado I passed a man sitting on a marble
bench chewing a lump of ice; he cracked off bits with his teeth
and crunched them noisily.

The Havana Hilton, the biggest hotel in Latin America, had
recently been renamed the Habana Libre, and a red banner reading
'We will conquer!' had been hung down the blue skyscraper. In
side its marble hall, hidden microphones dribbled non-stop music
recorded long ago by anonymous musicians in another world, and
a futuristic fountain dribbled non-stop water among a confection
of twisted bronze and fluorescent moss. At the bamboo bar sat a
few disconsolate Cubans, but the rows of souvenir shops were

15

utterly deserted. Groups of peasant girls, brought to the capital for a course in needlework, sat in the perpetual twilight, talking in the same subdued tone that the atmosphere cast upon everything, and porters with nothing to do lurked near the walls like sad phantoms. Against the stylized limb of a writhing concrete figure was propped a notice, 'Abolish illiteracy!' The huge Cadillac standing in the portico bore the arms of the Institute for Friendship with the Peoples, and three Russians in Oxford bags and Hawaiian shirts emerged from the lift hall and got into it.

In the casino some of the tables were still operating, and I stood to watch the beauty of the spinning roulette wheel, its dreadful revolutions silent except for the clacking of the ivory ball. But stakes were low, and there seemed to be no tension among the gamblers; the only pistols in sight were those of the two *milicianos* standing at the door, and the placard over the cashier, 'Lumumba will live for ever in the hearts of all free peoples,' served to bring to his senses any gambler tempted to stray too close to the brink of excess. Without its American tourists the hotel was reduced to its own silliness, a monument to a few brief seasons of gaiety and thoughtlessness.

*   *   *

In the Casa de las Americas, an institute for culture, there was a beautiful Spanish girl sitting alone in an office with deep arm-chairs and a sumptuous carpet. She wore fine American clothes, and her dark, mesmerizing eyes flashed from me to the papers and telephones on her desk, and out of the window to the sea.

'This morning my husband and I went and worked on a building site, where they are putting up flats for the people. You know—carrying bags of cement, mixing concrete, taking bricks to the work-men. It was hard. I had never done anything like that. Look at my hands!' She showed me the blisters on her lovely fingers and the chipped nail varnish. 'But now I feel so good. We achieved something. Not very much, perhaps, for the building; but for ourselves we learnt how a house is built, how a workman spends his day,

16

what it's like to be sweating in the sun, to breathe dust, to smile at a man who shares the same experience. And now, I feel so good,' and she wriggled a little.

It might have sounded priggish, but she was too beautiful.

*   *   *

It was marvellous to be hot. For a sensualist, the feeling of the sun-warmed air actually touching one's face, and of the cool patch at the back of the neck, moist with sweat, was delicious. The tall glasses of ice, filled up with rum and ginger ale—the rum pale and quite un-syrupy—were a pleasure for the evenings, and I never got tired of the bollo-bollo-bollo of Bacardí being poured from a bottle on to a lump of ice.

But at first I didn't like Havana as a city. It grew up to satisfy the annual swarm of American tourists, and now that they had all gone, it was left for the Cubans to rattle around in their big cars, like pimps in a brothel after all the customers have left. The longer I stayed, however, the more I grew to like it. One could forget the brash façade of a huge pleasure town, and even, for a moment, the equally unattractive countenance of a people in arms. Down at the harbour entrance, at night, fishermen cast their lines into the invisible water, and lovers sat in pairs along the sea wall, like surreptitious swallows. The beam of the Morro lighthouse revolving across the city flashed twice on each block of flats, and the white and red lights of the cars streamed along the curve of the Malecón. Suddenly a great ship would slip out of the night and into the harbour, the hammer and sickle illuminated on her funnel.

'Why, Havana's dead now!' wheezed an elderly British business-man. But it wasn't dead at all. It had just become more Cuban. The negroes sitting on the marble benches of the Prado, the children playing hopscotch under the trees, the hordes of peasant girls billeted in the big tourist hotels for courses in needlework—they were all living in their own city, and at last they had it to themselves. There were foreigners, of course—the new foreigners, from countries that had never before sent tourists to Cuba; and it was disconcerting at

17

first to have small boys calling out at me, 'Soviético! Soviético!' If I protested that I wasn't, they would go on guessing—Czech, Polish, German—until I told them I was English, but to them one European country was as remote as another. 'You speak English?' they would ask, and then be puzzled that I wasn't an American. Before the revolution, foreigners had meant only one thing.

The most important of the new foreigners at that time were the Chinese. A colossal China-can-make-it exhibition had been opened in the Palacio de Bellas Artes, and the people of Havana were lining up by the thousand to see it. At the entrance a team of milicianos searched everybody for hidden bombs, milicianas rummaged in women's handbags; and inside, beside every showcase and piece of machinery, sat a guard with a carbine across his knees. The favourite exhibit, after the Coca-Cola machine, was a big map of the world, showing Cuba; men stood in front of it, proudly pointing out their country to their wives and children, and explaining about the terrible distance to Peking and the much more terrible closeness of the United States. Outside the building, on the pavement, enterprising vendors were cashing in on the people's sudden passion for China and were selling Chinese rice bowls, soup spoons, fans and toys; nobody noticed that everything came from Hong Kong.

'Hey, mister! You wan' taxi?' Two men were sitting in the shade of an arcade; but when I walked past without answering, the one who had shouted turned to his companion: 'He don't speak English. He's a Russki.'

But most of the people who had made a living out of the tourists had now become too fossilized and too drugged by idleness even to shout. Occasionally I was struck by a desperate, 'Hi, sir, wha'dye know?' but it was uttered without conviction, almost unconsciously, like the last spasm of a dying body. Even the tarts no longer bothered one, and the only time I was accosted in the street it was a sort of apology, almost a joke. A huge black man came at me out of the night, and spoke in a deep voice, confidentially: 'I have a mos' beautiful girl I would like you to meet. Jus' two blocks from here. Come and meet her. What's that? Why don't I keep her for myself? Well, she's not really mine, see. She don' belong to me. She

18

won' cost you much. Oh, you don't? Well then, sure. But buy me a coffee, won't you? Jus' twenty cents.'

One evening I pushed through the upholstered leather door of a little night club, from the brilliant street lights into a cavernous murk. After a few seconds I saw a dim row of bottles reflecting the orange glimmer of the discreetest of lighting, and the glow of a monumental juke-box. I sat down at the bar and ordered a beer, but before it came I felt fingers running across my back and slipping under my arm, and there was Gloria on the next stool, her hand pressed into mine and her magnificent bosom quivering just below my nose.

There had once been fifty girls working in that club, she said, but now there were only seventeen, and they very rarely got anything to do. Last year Gloria and another girl had taken a trip abroad, to Mexico, Panama and Venezuela, where they had found temporary jobs in the local bars and brothels, but they had come back to Cuba, and now there was a law banning them from going away again.

With every whisky she drank Gloria became more stunningly beautiful, and her sticky little hand only left mine to run softly up to my neck and down to my knees. Suddenly the barman held up a ten-cent packet of soap flakes, and Gloria shrieked with delight. 'For my mother,' and she pulled out a fifty-cent piece. It was the first packet she had seen for three weeks. Onions were scarce too, she added.

'But the revolution's not my business. So I don't talk about it.'

Another night I went to the Tropicana, which had once been advertised as the world's most fabulous night club. At the entrance was a huge wooden arch with a banner saying, 'Welcome, comrade workers and *milicianos*!' but inside it was darker than it had been out in the starlit night. I groped through a succession of glass doors and found myself in a casino, with a few dilatory gamblers. I asked for the bar, and somebody pointed further into the darkness. Tripping over an electric flex, or it may have been a tropical snake, I crashed into a tall bar stool, and with a grunt of relief sat down on it and ordered a rum.

I was in the holy of holies, and as my eyes grew accustomed to the darkness I began to see just what kind of a shrine it was. It appeared to be a huge hangar built of glass and plaster, and gradually my eyes settled on familiar objects. There was a tree not far from me, an immense tropical vegetable, green and plaited, that writhed its way up to the roof; and somewhere in the murk I recognized the sleepy glint of an artificial rubber-plant. Over my head hung an enormous mobile, ready to drop. Or was it a palm tree? A face, dimly familiar, emerged from the darkness; whoever it belonged to, it was a comfort and I smiled at it—and saw it was my own, reflected in a hidden mirror.

In the far distance, about a quarter of a mile from me, was a stage with a band sitting on it and a small dance floor in front, on which three couples were dutifully shuffling. One girl was dressed like a debutante, another was dressed as a *miliciana* with a pistol in her belt, and the third was hardly dressed at all. There was none of the vitality and rhythm I had associated with Cuban music; half the musicians were violinists, and the noise they made suggested that the banner over their heads, ' The Pride of the People of Cuba ', had been put up by someone who had never heard them play. Very few of the tables were occupied, and there was only one other man sitting at the bar with me. He was a negro from Jamaica, and he was slightly drunk.

' Come here once-twice a month. Spend three-four dollars at the bar. See the show. Never been to a night club before the revolution. Look ! " The Pride of the People of Cuba ". It's ours now.'

Behind the bar, at the till, was an official from INIT, the National Institute of the Tourist Industry, sitting in profound idleness, yawning and combing his hair. He wore dark sunglasses to shield him from the glare of the little green and purple lights behind the bottles. Somebody in uniform, with long hair curling to the shoulders, came up to me with a collection box, for the Young Rebels. I wasn't sure whether it was a boy or a girl.

The deliberate tropical atmosphere was utterly spoilt by the cold, sterilized air-conditioning. I longed for fireflies, or even mosquitoes; and so far from sweating, I shivered on my little stool. Frank

Sinatra used to charge a thousand dollars a night to perform in the Tropicana. I would charge about that, too.

By the time the show began the place was almost half full, though it was obvious that most of the customers were not going to spend any money on food or drinks; they had just come for some free entertainment, and to see how the rich used to live. For an hour they sat and watched while a succession of singers strode backwards and forwards across the stage trailing a microphone on a long flex and pouring distorted, incoherent noises into it. There was a man dressed up like a dentist, and a woman with a great white pair of rabbit's ears on her head and nothing much else, and another man in black tails who kept tripping over the microphone flex while coloured lights revolved mercilessly round him. The lights all went off, and came on again to reveal three girls in crinolines alone on the stage, their backs to the audience; there was a roll of drums and a flourish of trumpets as the girls turned slowly round—but they had no crinolines in front. For silliness and vulgarity the show could scarcely have been excelled, but as a distraction on a dull evening at a holiday camp, or even duller one at a national teetotallers' convention, it might have passed; and the Tropicana was something between the two. At any rate, it seemed to please the customers, and they clapped uncritically at the end of every number.

The finale was an imitation of an early technicolour musical from Hollywood, with a tenth of the talent and without Betty Grable. Streams of girls with the same white rabbit's ears, white fluffy tails and white paws, but otherwise almost naked, converged on the stage from all corners of the building, carrying burning torches. Six terrifying bunnies popped up behind the bar where I was sitting and made little jabs at me with their front paws before scuttling off among the tables and up to the stage. When the stage was over-flowing with them—white bunny at their extremities and nude girl in between—a satin curtain was pulled back to reveal still more of them, with coloured spotlights picking out a green breast, a pink navel, a silver G-string, or casting a purple highlight on the swelling of a tummy. Far behind them all, on an arc spanning the sky between two clouds, wiggling their fluffy tails and throwing futile streamers over the heads of their sister bunnies, was the ultimate, inaccessible platoon—a rainbow of rabbits.

But there was not a scrap of eroticism in the whole show. The band and the singers drooled on, and the spectators, many of whom were in sunglasses, gawped with bewilderment. Only the Jamaican next to me at the bar, who had turned right round on his stool and sat cross-legged with his mouth open, uttering little gasps of ecstasy, seemed moved by the performance. The Tropicana was as chilly as its air-conditioning, a vast temple of frigidity.

*   *   *

Having been turned away from the Ministry of Foreign Affairs by a girl who was inundated by people clamouring for visas to leave Cuba, I went round to the Institute for Friendship with the Peoples. My name was taken, and I found myself in a waiting-room with a Canadian journalist, a Bolivian miner and a man from Colombia who said that he had once been a worker but was now a driver; in his blue suit and rimless glasses he looked like a prosperous American businessman, and he admitted that his bourgeois appearance was a great advantage, because all the counter-revolutionaries came up to him and poured out their troubles, which he then passed on to his friends at the Institute.

'This is history,' said the Canadian journalist. 'Real history, being played out in front of our eyes. I guess if I stay around a while longer it'll get even more historic.' He was sensational about the fighting that was going on in the Escambray mountains in central Cuba, and about the counter-revolutionary bombs that went off every night; within six months, he was certain, there would be civil war throughout Cuba. Six months? 'No,' he thought again. 'I give it two weeks.' Not so long after that, he himself was arrested by the G-2, the secret police, and spent an uneasy week under interrogation.

Eventually I was called into an inner office, and told that I would be given every possible facility to enable me to see every possible aspect of the revolution.

22

Sure enough, next morning I was picked up in one of the Institute's air-conditioned Cadillacs, in a corner of which reclined the benign and slightly cynical figure of a distinguished British socialist, and together we were whisked off on a conducted tour of East Havana, an unfinished city of apartment blocks overlooking the Gulf of Mexico. We were shown diagrams of the estate, with its shopping centre, hospital and school, and huge photographs of the grubby old market in Havana, chaotic and unhygienic, which had now been pulled down, and of the concrete supermarket, spacious and sterile, that was soon to be opened in the new suburb.

'And the fact,' said the distinguished British socialist a little nostalgically, 'that you and I would prefer to do our shopping in the old place is quite irrelevant.'

We were taken into a model apartment, already fitted with potted rubber-plants and reproductions of modern Cuban paintings, and told about the terrible slums that Cuban workers had lived in, in the days of imperialism. Now they were being given decent homes, with gas cooking-stoves, modern drains, baths and even bidets.

'All the women I've ever known,' said the distinguished British socialist still more nostalgically, 'have managed perfectly well without bidets.'

But after the tour of East Havana the Institute for Friendship with the Peoples must have decided, quite properly, that I was not one of the peoples they were supposed to be friendly with, for they never offered me any more outings. I didn't mind. The unreadable pamphlets they gave me, the meaningless statistics in the newspapers and the slogans in the streets, provided all the liturgy I needed; and an interview with a sanctimonious man in the Ministry of Foreign Affairs was so predictably tedious that I never bothered to ask for any more.

All Latin America, he said, had its eyes fixed on Cuba, and he preened himself at the thought. In other countries the people were still living in poverty, misery and oppression, as had the Cubans before their revolution, while their masters wallowed in riches controlled by the United States. But Cuba had set the pattern, and revolution would soon come to them all, adapted in each country

23

to suit the particular political, geographic and economic conditions. He couldn't say exactly when it would be, but until then Cuba was doing its best to help the various organizations—trades unions, women's associations, peace committees, youth leagues—that were working for revolution. Cuban embassies in Latin American capitals dispensed literature and suggestions, and invitations to visit the first *Territorio Libre de América*. That was the job of a foreign service. Embassies of all nations did it.

'But in Cuba we have found that the embassies of the socialist countries have been more useful to us than those of the capitalist ones. It's a pity.'

The most sympathetic person I met in any government department—as well as being one of the most loyal revolutionaries—was the office boy in the Ministry of Education, who came round with black coffee in a thermos flask which he sold for three cents in cups made of pieces of folded paper, like miniature paper boats. Across the boy's bottom, sewn to his pants under a sheet of cellophane, was the new cover picture of a Cuban-Soviet magazine, showing a coloured photograph of Castro and Khruschev embracing each other, cheek to cheek—one face on each buttock.

* * *

When, within a hundred yards of you, four different rumba bands are playing, a few dozen policemen are blowing whistles and three Buicks are blowing their horns, a girl is screaming because somebody has just emptied a bag of confetti down her bosom, six beer vendors are competing with six assorted bells, a horse is whinnying with sheer terror, a man in a window is yelling because he has spotted a girl friend going by on a float, a gang of boys are whizzing past on roller skates, a horrid kid is clutching your trousers and blowing a toy that makes a noise like three women being strangled in the dark, and half a million Cubans are revelling in their special Cuban way, it is hard to keep up the proper phlegm expected of an Englishman abroad.

It was the first day of the Havana carnival, and at about nine o'clock in the evening Fidel Castro appeared at the front of a stand outside the Capitol, shaking hands benevolently with everybody within reach. Photographers smothered him, television flood lamps drenched him, but he came up smiling every time. The crowd—but to call it simply the crowd is to convey no idea of its density or its exuberance—set up a chant, ' *Fi-DEL! Fi-DEL! Fi-DEL!* ' which continued until an army motor-cycle display was announced over the loudspeakers. Though it sounded more suitable for a military tattoo than a carnival, it was a reminder that Cuba was not only in a state of revolution but was officially expecting any day to be invaded. The riders had ' *Team acrobático* ' written on their shirts, and the motor-bikes, of course, were made in the country from where the invasion was expected.

When they had roared away there was a lull, and a little man in baggy trousers came out and stood in the middle of the road, shouted for attention, and began his own acrobatics, turning somer-saults on the tarmac, leaping in the air, shooting across the road in a string of cart-wheels in front of Castro's stand. He was far better than the motor-bikes, and everybody knew it. A soldier with a car-bine half-heartedly tried to stop him, but the crowd wanted the little man, and they clapped and cheered. Castro was studiously talking to his neighbour, and a party from the Russian embassy—solid, grey-suited men, fat blonde women and pale children—looked uncom-fortable.

After his performance, the private acrobat went and sought an interview with Castro. He was granted it, and the crowd cheered again as he talked to the bearded *Máximo Líder* over the edge of the stand, man to man. Castro was approachable. Anyone could have had a word with him, asked his opinion, or given him advice. And anyone, for that matter, could have shot him.

Then came the floats, gigantic juggernauts aglitter with neon and tinsel, blaring music from hidden gramophones and pulled by jeeps. They were mostly contributed by government departments and trades unions, and were allegorical not of bounty or spring or love, but of industrialization, education, commerce, transport, and all the dreary symptoms of a self-conscious government. On each float, dressed more or less in the appropriate uniform—or if nothing seemed appropriate, then dressed in almost nothing—and wiggling to the inaudible rhythm of a rumba, was a troupe of girls. With one hand they steadied themselves on a piece of glittering cardboard, and with the other they flung streamers at the crowd. And all the time they went on wiggling. I wondered what the Russians made of all that wiggling.

At the back of every float, on the tailboard, sat a *miliciano*, with a crate of fizzy drinks beside him and a rifle across his knees—just to remind us of the counter-revolution in our midst. But the idea of a bomb being thrown at those tireless, laughing, wiggling girls was too terrible to think of.

By the time the Queen herself appeared, the centre of Havana was a teeming, squealing mass of people and paper, so thick that it would seem impossible for anyone to move. But men were somehow squeezing through, selling funny hats, beer, ices, peanuts, oranges, ham rolls, whistles; policemen were shouting and waving their arms; and boys were throwing confetti over every pretty girl they saw, and brushing it into their hair with paper whisks. For such a tight crowd it was surprising how much movement there was. The mass was liquid.

The Queen's procession was led by a man in silver tights, carrying two outspread wings like an immense vampire; behind him came unicorns, oxen and a giant dressed like the King of Hearts, followed by hundreds of attendants with silver fans. The royal carriage, pulled by an invisible jeep buried below an orchestra of golden harps and trumpets, was so vast that it scarcely fitted into the street. It was like a moving mountain rising from the foothills at the front through glaciers and snowfields to the final peak, where reigned the Queen. Above her head floated two white swans, and behind her throne rose a tremendous star-burst, its silver prongs reaching out to the gutters and above the trees to the rooftops. On every silver glacier sat a silver princess, laughing a silver laugh and tossing streamers to the crowd. Not quite so fairy-like was the man in dungarees who dashed up and down the mountain range attending to the electric wiring. But the Queen herself was all a Queen

26

should be. Like royalty she smiled, and waved a sickly hand. Poor girl, she looked tired, and someone had passed her up a Coca-Cola.

Then came the *comparsas*, the troupes of dancers, ecstatic, phrenetic, dancing up the street, each with its own band—a few drummers and percussion players, a couple of trumpeters—shuffling along in a tight little bunch behind. Dancing, dancing—laughing, sweating, sometimes singing—but always dancing. A monstrous scarlet telephone, rolling along with a leggy girl perched foolishly in every finger-hole of the dial, gave out a pathetic pop, and stopped; its lights and music went out, and all night it stood like a wreck while the tide of dancers streamed past, lost in their own ecstasy. Joy it was, sheer joy; and the crowd too went wild. Starlings shrieked in the trees, astonished but unheard.

I have a vision of an exotic flock of birds with emerald and purple ostrich plumes performing some delirious mating act as they danced up the street; of a ragged band of drums and trumpeters so compulsive that all the negroes in the crowd joined in behind them, their arms and legs flailing, their bottoms jerking and their eyeballs bursting; of a Spanish aristocrat dripping with paper, lifting his silver trumpet far above the din and playing a salvo to the moon; of an old black man with a monkey and a wooden leg, leaning on his crutch and waving his stump in the air as he danced; and of an old black woman in a crinoline rumba-ing up the street, clutching in her hand a bottle of beer and in her teeth a huge cigar.

More and more the crowd surrendered to individualism, and the streets became filled with Harlequins, Don Quixotes, teams of horsemen, cowboys, carriages bursting with ladies in pink and gold dresses, black men, white men, yellow men, red men, blue men, men fifteen feet tall, men with four legs, men with no heads, men with two heads, and men with things that men don't normally have at all. The decline of the official side to the carnival only marked the triumph of the people; the Coca-Cola stalls and juke-boxes set up in the street, the confetti and fancy dresses in the crowd, were as ritualistic as the frenzied movements of the dancers and the fantastic symbols dragged out from the darkness of a half-remembered past.

27

It was a pageant of glory and magic and awe, a night of noise and wonder. As the last troupe passed for the last time, the crowd broke through behind it, knocked over the chairs and the policemen, and danced through their city to bed. And the next night they did it all again.

*   *   *

The catholic church put up a poster all over Cuba showing the face of a small, rather pretty boy, staring into the future with the innocence of a chorister. ' Will he be brought up as a Believer or an Atheist? It's up to you. Teach him the catechism.'

Very soon, another identical poster appeared everywhere, showing the same boy. ' Will he be brought up as a Patriot or a Traitor? It's up to you. Teach him to co-operate.'

*   *   *

' Jesus. That's right; Jesus. Like Jesus Christ, but just Jesus. Lots of Cubans are called Jesus. Listen, friend. You my friend, aren't you? Hey, two beers! Listen, friend. Batista was the cause of the revolution. Without Batista there would never be a revolution. Listen, you want to change dollars? Listen, at the bank you get one dollar one peso. Listen, my friend, I give you two pesos. You got dollars? Well, I give you two pesos. I'm a taxi-driver. Look, here's my licence. Only for three months; it used to be two years. That's my social security card. I worked in Chicago once. I been everything; shoe-shine, everything. Listen, you my friend. I'm psychologic. Some foreigners, they work for the government. I talk to them, they take me to the *tribunal*. How you say *tribunal*? That's it, law court. Politics. But you my friend. I trust you. Listen, you give me dollars, I give you two pesos. Okay? Okay, okay. Hey, two beers! You like Cuban beer? Three kinds, Hatuey, Polar, Cristal. But all the same now. No difference. Nationalized. I got six sons. Yeah, six sons. I'm fifty-five. Look, here's my insurance card. Born 1911. What? I know, I know, but I say I'm fifty-five. Where you want
28

to go tomorrow? Trades Unions? That! They only give you all the communist crap. You want to listen to me. Look, I got six sons. Six wives. Sure, six wives. In Cuba, live with a girl, have a baby. Easy. I got a lovely bambino, eight months. I'm fifty-five. Hell, I only do it once a night, but boy! when I do it. Lovely bambino, eight months. Hey, two beers! I'm fifty-five. Listen, you give me one dollar, I give you two pesos. Okay? Okay, okay. You my friend. I give you two-fifty. You got cash? Or traveller's cheques? I give you two-fifty. Listen, I been taxi-driver thirty-five years. Not one accident. Yeah, thirty-five years. Sure, I know Cuba. Where you want to go? Listen, I not made a dollar for two years now. I used to earn ten-twenty dollars a day. I had three thousand dollars in the bank. Tomorrow I show you my bank book. Three thousand dollars. Now, I got, maybe thousand five hundred, thousand six hundred. I spend hundred dollars a month. Apartment, beautiful apartment I got. Three rooms. Beautiful. I used to pay sixty dollars a month. Now I pay thirty. They cut the rent, after the revolution. Then I pay laundry, food, gasoline for the car. I got radio, television, telephone. I got everything. But I don't make anything now. What do I do when there's nothing in the bank? Don't know, don't know. Maybe I put a revolver here. Maybe. And I drink. I don't eat. I don't like to eat. But I drink. And I smoke. Hey, two beers! You like this beer? Sure, but they're all the same now. Nationalized. Listen, I been everywhere. Panama, Mexico, Miami, everywhere. Listen, I give you two-fifty pesos one dollar. Okay? Okay, okay. How much you got? Hey, how much you got? Okay. My biggest boy, he's a technician. He gets ten-twelve dollars a day. That's fine. That's fine for the young. But I not make anything. Not for two years now. I'm not saying anything. I don't know anything. I not bought a newspaper for a year and a half. I don't know anything. Newspapers, they're all the same now. Three newspapers every morning, *Revolución*, *Hoy*, *El Mundo*. But they're all the same. Like the beer. But three papers, see? Sure, it's good for young people. I don't mind, I don't mind. Listen, I pay four dollars insurance. What I get? I get a funeral. But I'm not dead. I'm fifty-five. I think I got ten years. Listen, you my friend. Hey, two beers! That guy

29

there is always drunk. He won five thousand dollars month ago on the lottery. Now he's always drunk. They still call it the lottery. But it's sort of bonds. The carnival? You should've seen it fifteen-twenty years ago. I don't know what it is. It's not politics. No, the carnival's not politics. Maybe the people happier then, twenty years ago. Before Batista. He started it. Without Batista there would never be a revolution. All those girls in the carnival. You like them? Just girls. From the whore houses. Pretty quiet now, the whore houses. You should see my bambino. Eight months. I'm fifty-five. I not do it often now. Just once, understand? But when I do it, boy! I got a lovely bambino. Listen, you my friend. One day, you come and eat my place. You my friend. Hey, two beers! Listen, listen. I give you two-fifty, hell no, I give you three pesos one dollar. Okay? Okay, okay. Never mind. You, me, friends. I understand. Hell no, I not understand.'

*   *   *

In Cuba there is a thing called a *bola*. During those months of jitteriness and apprehension which ended with the invasion fiasco in April 1961 another bomb went off almost every night in Havana, and almost every morning another *bola*, that special Cuban squib, exploded. Whoever let it off, it was passed red-hot over the telephone lines between newspaper offices and embassies, or tossed non-chalantly among the murky characters hovering at the bar of the *Gato Tuerto*, the One-Eyed Cat. In there, with terrible lurid paintings just discernible on the walls, and a piano so invisible in the darkness that one never thought of its pianist, but just of the piano playing sadly to itself, and sometimes a wailing female voice, equally disembodied, and the plop and chink of rum on ice—in the *Gato Tuerto* the *bolas* fairly sizzled. At the bar I once heard an Irishman talking Italian to a Yugoslav, who was answering in Spanish; every sentence of their conversation was a *bola*.

Bolas were topical, or irrefutable, or laughable, or improbable, or unprintable, but never quite impossible, and in their heyday they came thick and fast: two Russian submarines had been seen in

30

Santiago harbour; the holes that were being dug in the ground near Pinar del Río were not for eucalyptus trees at all, but for missiles; the shortage of beer in the bars was because the new bottle tops that had arrived from Czechoslovakia didn't fit the old bottles; all paper money was quite worthless; President Dorticós had been caught trying to flee to Miami disguised as a nun; Fidel was spending his nights at the Chinese embassy; on the contrary, Fidel was spending his nights at Celia's.

Sometimes the government itself was rumoured to have launched a well-timed *bola*—but that, of course, was merely another *bola*. 'We must be prepared for Yankee *bolas*,' shouted the evening paper. And just as the nightly explosion that rumbled across Havana turned out, as often as not, to be only the nine o'clock cannon that had been fired regularly at La Cabaña fortress since the days of the Spanish empire, so the newest *bola* tended to be too easily explained away. Havana was a city of rumours and calumny, and *bolas* were the bread of an uncertain and precarious life.

*　　　*　　　*

One day in March 1960 a French ship, *La Coubre*, with a cargo of arms and explosives from Belgium, blew up in Havana harbour, killing a number of French sailors and Cuban dock workers. The Cuban government, without hesitation, accused the United States of sabotage, and all sorts of unanswerable reasons were produced to prove that the explosion could only have been planned by American agents when *La Coubre* was being loaded in Antwerp. Fidel Castro went down to the docks while the wrecked ship was still smouldering and made one of his most histrionic speeches, which was such a success that a year later, on the first anniversary of the explosion, he decided to do it again.

The speech was announced for three o'clock on Sunday afternoon, but nobody really expected anything to begin before six, and the long hot hours were spent by thousands of Cubans in the fun of the fair—buying beer, Coca-Cola, straw hats, peanuts, and little sugary things of every conceivable unattractiveness. The one-man stallkeepers did tremendous business, but the people who did best of all out of the occasion were the florists and wreath-makers. Groups of workers and militia men and women marched down to the docks carrying huge bouquets, trailing with ribbons and banners, which they laid round a monstrous concrete monument that had been erected for the victims, topped with a lump of twisted, rusty iron salvaged from *La Coubre*. Very soon the lump of iron, the monument and the little ornamental pool of water at its foot were obliterated by flowers.

There was a platform with microphones put up in the middle of a wide space between the dockyard buildings, and opposite it a battery of television cameras and loud-speakers, but the only real sign that the performance was to be given by the *Máximo Líder* himself was the quantity of armed militia men and women everywhere. Along all the warehouse roofs, in every window of every building around, up in the trees, on balconies, and even patrolling along the tops of the goods wagons in the railway sidings, were men and women in uniform, with guns. And among the crowd, too, they wandered quietly, their fingers just touching their triggers and their muzzles pointed always into my face. All those muzzles, and all those fingers on all those triggers.

As the crowd thickened it became so hot standing in the glare of the whitewashed dockyard buildings that I was driven to the shade of an adjoining square, where people were selling orange juice and coconuts under the trees, and where there was even room to lie down on the grass. I wandered about taking photographs, particularly of a platoon of *milicianas*. They were an enthralling collection, ranging from frustrated, grey-haired women standing toughly with their legs apart, chewing oranges and smoking cigarettes, to teenage girls who were paying too much attention to their eye-shadow and none at all to where their carbines were pointing. They all wore the black skirts and khaki shirts of *miliciana* uniform, and some of them were very alluring indeed; but whereas most of them were in hobnail boots a few were in elegant little shoes with stiletto heels, which made them quite ridiculously pretty. When a girl soldier takes the trouble to discard her clumsy boots for something more

32

flimsy, one's faith in femininity is half restored; and fully restored when she carries, as well as her rifle, a parasol.

In charge of this platoon was a stalwart sergeant with a huge bosom and a searing voice, who waddled among her flock cracking jokes and . . .

I had never heard machine-gun fire before. But I was not a bit surprised. In fact, though the shooting started so suddenly, it seemed so absolutely natural that I felt just tremendously relieved. Of course, it was obvious: this was what we had all come for. Now we should not have to hang around waiting any longer. But what did surprise me, and frighten me too, was the behaviour of the people round me. Men began to shout, and women began to scream. And everybody pulled their triggers.

'Down! Down!' yelled someone, and they all dropped to the ground. The *milicianas* were flattened round me, and I found myself standing there alone, like a lighthouse in a sea of prostrate, screaming women. The view opened up, and I saw across the square a black and yellow taxi racing in front of the warehouses and down into a side street. Vaguely I realized that it had something to do with the shooting, and even more vaguely I realized that I should be taking photographs, not just standing there. My camera was open, but the decision whether to point it at the disappearing taxi or at the screaming women was too much for such a crowded moment. Bullets were cracking everywhere.

Suddenly I found myself lying on the ground among the *milicianas*. I looked up and saw soldiers running across the road and crouching under the shelter of a row of Russian lorries that had been unloaded from a ship.

'*Disciplina! Disciplina!*' shrieked the woman sergeant above the screams, but it made no difference.

'Heads down!' shouted a man, and the girls screamed louder.

But the taxi had already gone and the firing was over, except for a few happy shots. Immediately began the stampede. The crowd rushed across the road, howling, and the *milicianas*, now that there were no more bullets to scream about, got up from the ground and

RR—B

screamed about themselves. Suddenly one of them had an idea : the firing-squad.

'*Paredón!*' They all set up a great diabolical chant. '*Pa-re-DÓN! Pa-re-DÓN!*' It was a terrifying, atavistic sight—a band of women and girls howling for a man's blood—and my first reaction was simply to stand appalled, feeling sick. My second reaction was to try to take a photograph.

But there was too much going on in too many places for me to be able to concentrate on any subject for long enough to focus the camera. Men shouted and rushed about poking guns through windows and behind trees, bullets occasionally cracked like forgotten squibs, an ambulance that appeared in the square blowing its horn crashed into one of the Russian lorries and was wrecked, half the crowd began to stream down the side street where the taxi had disappeared, and the women went on yelling for blood : '*Pa-re-DÓN!*'

The papers next morning carried the full story: 'When the counter-revolutionaries' shots were first heard, the people gave a beautiful example of valour and serenity. Some lay on the ground, others remained standing. But nobody moved from his place, nobody thought of escaping, nobody let himself be overtaken by panic, which would have been a thousand times more dangerous than the bullets. Men and women, old and young, simply did their duty, demonstrating once again our national decision to face all risks with a brave heart and a calm spirit.' Hurrah ! I too was much more frightened by the screaming women than by the bullets.

When everything was over and the crowd had gone back to its Coca-Cola and orange juice, there were two pools of blood on the tarmac near the line of Russian lorries.

It was nearly time for the speeches, and the military precautions were intensified. More and more men appeared with guns along the rooftop skylines, and a wide passage was cleared leading to the platform. The television men climbed up the scaffolding to their cameras, and the loudspeakers were tested. The *milicianas*, tired of shouting but proud of their performance, tweaked their uniforms into shape and touched up their eye-shadow again.

34

A cheer went up and a young man in a blue suit with long hair and a boyish face was quick-marched by an escort of soldiers to the platform. A few people who recognized him clapped, and he grinned and waved back before hurrying up the ladder and taking a seat near the microphones. An old woman near me who was clapping feverishly said that he was the Minister of Education, and the best they had ever had, and she nodded with happiness and clapped even harder.

Another car drove up and a more typical leader, in uniform with a beard, stepped out. It was the head of INRA, the National Institute for Agrarian Reform, who had been a professor of geography before the revolution. The line of *milicianos* standing shoulder to shoulder along the clear passage to the platform turned their backs on him and faced the crowd, half scowling, half smiling.

Then there was a long pause while we waited for the *Máximo Líder*. A motor-bike raced up and down the cleared passage, and we peered over the *milicianos* to see him arrive. Suddenly a shout went up from the other end of the crowd, and we turned round. Castro and President Dorticós were already mounting the platform; to fox us they had come by boat and landed at the quay where *La Coubre* had exploded. The band played the national anthem, and the crowd shouted, ' *Fi-DEL! Fi-DEL! Fi-DEL!* '

The first speech was by a French trades unionist, and nobody understood a word of it until he came to something which sounded familiar—*impérialisme, soviétique, Yankees*—or which could be recognized as part of a slogan, when they all cheered madly. After him came a Cuban, who produced a masterpiece of the brutal, crowd-exciting technique, starting with low, sombre sob-stuff about the victims of *La Coubre*, and ending on a wild shriek.

Then came Castro. He stepped to the microphones, and they all began to roar. They roared for ten minutes. He stood there, fiddling with the microphones, looking tough but also tired, and infinitely sad. Perhaps he was sad. Perhaps he had been told about the two pools of blood. Perhaps things weren't going right. Perhaps he was just overworked. Perhaps he had sold them all down the river. The Moscow river. He had a hunted look, as he stood in front of them,

35

adjusting and re-adjusting the microphones and clasping and un-clasping his hands. But the crowd roared on. Old women stood up on their seats and shrilled their adulation, tears rolling down their cheeks; and people near me in the crowd watched to see how I was taking it.

There seemed no chance of the roar ending until somebody hit on the idea of playing the national anthem a second time. It imme-diately silenced the crowd, and when the last chord was still sound-ing, before they had time to start again, Castro began. 'Workers! Friends! Today . . .'

It was a tirade against the United States ('*Cuba sí, Yankees no!*' yelled the crowd), and then against the catholic priests ('*Para los curas, pa-re-DÓN*'), and it lasted four hours. He had no notes, but that is not why he repeated himself. Every sentence he twisted round and presented in three or four different ways, so that the point could be grasped by the dullest in the audience, and every time they cheered. The beard and the beret, the revolver holster, the jack-boots, the heroic gestures and the little nervous fiddlings with the microphones—was he a demagogue, a statesman, an orator, a pirate? One thing was evident: he was loved.

And he was tireless, too, this Prime Minister. Next morning he was a hundred miles away, cutting sugar cane with the peasants. And afterwards, on his way back to Havana, he stopped off at a co-operative farm for a game of pelota.

*   *   *

Hortensia Droop was her name, and she looked as improbable as she sounded. I met her in the Palacio de Bellas Artes, where for the first time since arriving in Cuba I was frisked for weapons by the sentry; without getting up from his chair or taking his cigar out of his mouth, he ran his hands up to my arm-pits and down my trouser legs. It was all the more humiliating for being performed in a building devoted to culture, and when the sentry had finished with me I was in no condition to be polite to Señorita Droop. She had her feet up on a settee in the waiting-room, and she was wearing
36

a threadbare cape and a grubby handkerchief over her head. There were greasy fingerprints on her dark glasses.

'I know England,' she said, wiping her hand across her nose. 'I was at school at Eastbourne.' She kicked her shoes off on to the floor and began rubbing her ankles, whistling slightly through her teeth as though she were rubbing down a horse. 'I've written sketches of many famous Englishmen. Churchill, for instance, I sent it to him, and he wrote back. And Montgomery.' Then she put her shoes on again and leaned towards me. 'You see how frightened they are getting. All these sentries. They're terrified. It wasn't like this a year ago; not even two months ago. But now they've got the wind up.' I could hear the Eastbourne schoolgirl talking. 'It won't last long now. I give it a couple of months, no more. Everyone's against them.'

The official whom she was waiting to see came out of an office and she rushed for him, whooping as she must once have done on a Sussex hockey field. He swatted at her like a mosquito. I suppose every revolution has its Hortensia Droops, grumbling away their lives and believing to the last that it will all revolve back again.

Less pathetic, but more frightening because she had lived in Cuba for thirty years doing a job directly connected with politics, was an American woman journalist. I went to see her in her office, with a parrot and a cat crawling among the typewriters and ticker-tape machines. 'Well, they've done a damn marvellous job destroying the country's economy in only two years. Now, just take the example of the boy who washes my car every morning. Well, his mother . . .' And I listened to a story which perhaps concerned the car, or even the parrot, but certainly not the country's economy.

Carlitos, who owned a small perfume shop, was much more realistic. He had suffered badly from the drying-up of the tourist trade, and his Spanish wife's parents had even sent him an air ticket for the whole family to fly to Madrid, but he had decided to stay on in Cuba. His father had once owned a part share in a big sugar estate, and his mother used to draw eight thousand dollars a month from the rent of her twelve houses in Havana. Now the sugar industry was nationalized, and the tenants of the houses paid their rents, which had been cut in half, to the government; only six hundred dollars a month were passed to the old lady. Life was bitter for that generation.

But the revolution, said Carlitos, had at least taught the rich humility, and unselfishness—lessons which they had taken all too long to learn. 'When I have no business left, then I shall have to work for the state.' Meanwhile he had his collection of macabre literature and pornography to take his mind off things, and he had just finished writing an erotic novel. He didn't miss the tourists at all, even if it was bad for the shop. 'Cuba was like America's little child. Her favourite daughter. And when she ran away, America was mortified.' Then he thought for a moment, and smiled. 'But of course it was the Americans who were the children.'

A newspaper boy came into the bar where we were sitting and began shouting the headlines of the evening paper. A *miliciano* cursed him, and chased him out.

'Why shouldn't he sell his papers in here?' said Carlitos.

There must be many people like Carlitos, who are profoundly patriotic—but not to the extent of carrying revolvers—and deeply disillusioned with the past. They admire Castro, and though they have no great love for communism they hate the alternative. They want something new, and something Cuban.

'I hate uniforms,' said a film critic, a Spaniard who had come to Cuba after the revolution and taken Cuban citizenship. But he was already beginning to wonder. In Cuba there is no place for the cynic, let alone for the critic; still less is there a place for the rebel— the word rebel, adopted by the government, has been perpetuated until it simply means orthodox. An anti-rebel is a counter-revolutionary. And for those who forget, there is always La Cabaña fortress, brooding like a threat across the harbour, a reminder of the hundreds of men languishing inside, of the summary trials and sentences, of the executions at the *paredón* in the old dried-up moat. Everyone knows it's there, but they don't talk about it much, and when they do, they treat it as a joke and try to make it funny. Or else they dramatize it, and tell stories about the courage of the young men imprisoned there; about a youth, for instance, who by

38

shaving and cutting his hair short, managed to make himself look even younger than he was, and then wandered through the passages of the fortress asking to be shown the way out. He told the guards that he was his own younger brother, on a visit with a parcel of food and cigarettes, and that he had lost his way. He made it sound as though he was a little simple in the head, and in the end they led him to the gates and were glad to be rid of him.

The thing that appalled the film critic most of all was the lack of integrity among so many people—people who had shouted their praise of the Batista regime, and now shouted their praise of this. The editor of the communist newspaper, a leading Party member, had once been a member of Batista's government; and film critics who had been accustomed to praising all the trash from Hollywood that had been shown in Cuba, now did the same with the new Russian films, most of which were trash too; a journalist who had been a vigorous advocate of Castro and a denouncer of American imperialism fled from Cuba to the United States, where he became a vigorous journalist of quite another colour.

There are rats in every society, and this last one was by reputation a most unpalatable character. But what surprised me was not that one man should be guilty of such duplicity and immorality, but that he should have been considered as nothing very unusual, and that the existence was recognized of thousands of others like him, who were liable to behave in just the same way.

*   *   *

It is a revolution of the young; of people who are tired of the old cycle of revolutions that amounted to nothing more than presidential take-overs; who are weary of being the servants of American businessmen and the pimps of American tourists; who aspire to dignity, and to a national identity. But the lack of any precedent, and of any very articulate policy, accentuated the discomfort of their predicament; for tossed between the monster empires of Washington and Moscow, with feelings of public hate and private sympathy for one, and of public adoration and private awe for the

39

other, Cubans found themselves in a curious dilemma. From being so shamelessly American they had switched to being proudly anti-American. At least, however, they knew about the United States; many of them had been educated there, and many more had visited it or worked in it. Russia, on the other hand, was on the far side of the world, a great unknown land of snow and commissars and collective farms; and China was even further.

The expensive yacht clubs, the smart country clubs and private beaches had been nationalized and opened to the public. The huge abandoned houses of the rich Cubans who had fled to Miami had been sealed up by the National Institute for Urban Reform, or used for billeting homeless workers. The ' people' had become masters of a country hitherto selfishly attuned to the ' person'.

It was exciting, of course, so long as one didn't suffer personally too much. Iconoclasm is always fun. And to begin with it was all pretty easy. Cuba was a rich country, with enough land for everybody, much of which had never been worked properly. It merely needed ploughing up and planting with one of the many crops that had previously been imported from the United States. The wheels were going round, too, for there had been no devastating civil war across Cuba before the revolution.

Here was the chance—Cuba's chance, and America's chance. The squalid round of regimes born in violence, spent in corruption and selfishness, destroyed in more violence, was at last broken. Here was something new, patriotic, youthful, proud and jealous; something at first tender, but with roots in truth, and in the hearts of the people. This was not another palace revolution, another thunder-clap far above the heads of the people. This was a demonstration of man's desire to live in freedom in his own country, on his own land, under his own sky.

Cuba seized the chance, but America, to whom things un-American are things anti-American, was affronted. America shouted, and Cuba paid no attention. America turned her back, and Cuba, who badly needed help, went to the only other place where she could find it. America's bluff had been called, and if she lost any dignity in the eyes of Latin America it was because of her own blindness to nationalism, and to other people's preference for making a mess of their own affairs rather than having them properly looked after by strangers. Her final mistake was to be surprised.

It is another dictatorship, but for the first time the Cubans have a dictator who is not salting away a fortune in Swiss banks, and whom they shamelessly adore. Fidel—nobody calls him Castro—eats in public restaurants, takes advice from fishermen and gives it to villagers, and goes out to cut cane on Sundays. For the first time the people feel they have rulers whom they can treat as friends, and if at times there is a suspicion that the government doesn't seem to know exactly what they will do next, nobody blames them. For after all, who would expect a team of young men, none of whom could be described as professionals, to do any better? Running a country without any experience is not only a hazardous experiment, it's also a big adventure, and in Cuba the people genuinely feel involved in it; they are going somewhere, and they are getting there on their own. There is an amateurishness in Cuba that would be frightening if it were not so enthusiastic. It is exciting to discover one's own country, to feel ownership of it, and not only a sense of belonging but also a sense of possessing, and with it a responsibility. The best way to learn how to run a country, after all, is to try it and see.

Some people, of course, feel that it has gone too far, that it has swallowed its promises and that they have been betrayed. For a nation that in its richer classes has been so thoroughly American-ized, it has been difficult to reject the American way of life in favour of the austerity that they have always associated with communism. They have been so dazzled and bemused by American glitter and prosperity that they cannot easily renounce them. The desire for a national identity independent of America and the craving to be Cuban are balanced by an inescapable admiration for the United States—a passion that only aggravates the Cuban complex.

'Society is breaking up,' said a woman, half Cuban and half American, who had once been married to a Nazi and who was now working fervently for INRA. She felt that the old order, with a minority of haves, who had everything in the world, and a majority of have nots, who had nothing at all, was in ruins, and even though there was a new pseudo-communist government in charge there was no communist society. She admitted that a lot of people had bene-fited, and that the peasants and workers were better off than before, with more money, more work, more hospitals, more education. But instead of being inspired with unity and purposefulness, the people were only bewildered and disillusioned; and in the face of such efficiency they had become cynical as well. The only enthusiasm she had found in the country was not for communism but for Fidel. 'Cuba is communist,' she said, 'but being Cuban it simply hasn't paid its subscription.'

Nobody regrets the flight of the millionaires, for almost to a man they used their money for selfish purposes in a country where people were starving. The Cuban liberation which they shout about so much is not only liberation from the United States, but also from themselves, and from their own past; for Batista too was a Cuban. But the country itself was rich—indeed the rich men had got their riches from it—and it only needed a little selfless leader-ship and organization for the people too to benefit. That such necessities as agrarian reform, the ploughing up of virgin land, the planting of fruit and vegetables which had never been grown in Cuba before, the expansion of the rice fields, the big housing projects in the towns, the organization of labour and the first hesitant plans for light industry—that these should have had to wait for what one person called a break up of society and another the destruction of the economy, is no cause for the thousands of Cubans in Miami, or for that matter the millions in Cuba, to be proud. And it meant that because they came so late, they were accompanied by all the horrid things—the uniforms, the indoctrination classes, the stamp-ings and rantings, the bulging prisons, and the *paredón*.

II

Cuba: The Rest

THE CARRETERA CENTRAL RUNS THE LENGTH OF Cuba, a six-hundred-mile long ribbon of traffic, like an electric element threaded through the country, with the current switched on. Immense American diesel trucks roar along it, carrying sugar cane, cattle, bananas, cotton, and burning Russian fuel. Silver air-conditioned coaches (but now the air-conditioning is controlled by opening or closing the windows) hurtle between Havana and Santiago de Cuba, a bruising fifteen-hour journey. Herds of cattle amble along the tarmac, with real cowboys cracking whips, their lassos coiled on the pommels of their saddles.

The petrol stations have all had their capitalist badges removed, or painted over with the green and white colours of the nationalized oil industry; occasionally, through the new paint, one sees traces of the unmentionable word Esso, or the sinister outlines of a shell. And to emphasize the change, the new owners have put up a few of their own advertisements. 'To die for your country is to live,' they tell you, in colossal lettering. 'And you? What are you doing for your country? Join the militia !' commands a girl, pointing out of a poster like Kitchener in another world. But not everything is so earnest, and alongside the girl is a smaller, hand-painted notice, 'Exquisitos hot dogs.'

But the Carretera Central is like the Grand Trunk Road in Kim. Step down from the tarmac strip, walk a few yards along a rutted side-track, and you are in the Cuba of the last century, and the century before. The huge-wheeled ox carts are the same, and some of the sugar-stands, too, are said to have been planted in the days of the conquistadors. Only the highway, cutting across the plains and through the hills, ruthlessly chaining its travellers to a strip a

43

few yards wide and hundreds of cruel, sun-scorched miles long, has changed since Cortes' time.

There is another feature of the *Carretera Central* which is reminiscent of India. Every village, and every tiny settlement, has its shrine. But surprisingly there are no joss-sticks burning in it, and instead of the figure of Vishnu, or Ganesh, it is dedicated to the Apostle; a whitewashed altar supports the head of José Martí, cut off below the jaw and tilted forwards, his chin resting on the plinth. And all along the *Carretera*, painted on the barriers where the road is being mended, on walls and bridges, are samples of Martí's wisdom : 'To know how to read is to know how to work.' 'The most exhausting occupation is idleness.'

Apart from the mountains in the two end provinces of the island, Pinar del Río and Oriente, the Cuban countryside is not beautiful. Sugar is an unattractive crop at all seasons, and the rich plains of Matanzas, Las Villas and Camaguey provinces, in the centre of Cuba, make dull country. Camaguey has been hit hardest by the nationalizing zeal of the Cuban government, and its big sugar estates, rice farms, cattle ranches and orange groves have all been expropriated and converted into co-operatives or state farms.

Camaguey city, after Havana, is a lethargic place. There are the same shops full of models, the marble pavements, and neon signs, but church bells ring in the morning and there is none of the hectic brashness of the capital; the people of Camaguey are traditionally silent, content and lazy. In the men's clubs, as in Spain, the members sit in their rocking-chairs under oil paintings of their predecessors, chatting, smoking cigars, playing dominoes or dreaming. And in the cool of the arcades, fat old men sit up on high chairs all day, having their shoes polished and looking out glazedly into the sunshine. There are huge, elaborate barber's shops, and deserted beauty salons, and on the top floor of the Grand Hotel the Rotarians have their monthly lunch and make their sad, incredulous speeches. For a while they swam against the current, but some gave up and were swept hopelessly downstream, and the rest are now stranded, flapping and gasping.

But Camaguey has another, discordant characteristic which

makes it faintly like a town in the wild west. Dashing young men in cowboy hats, with pistols and high-heeled boots, who look convincingly as though they have left their horses tied to a post at the end of the street, swagger out of saloon bar doors and whistle at the girls.

*   *   *

I was to have been picked up at eight in the morning at the Grand Hotel. At nine-thirty someone telephoned to say that they would be along in half an hour, and at eleven they arrived—two *milicianos*.

'This is Cuban time,' said one of them cheerfully, but the other was deadly earnest. They took me off in a taxi to the town hall where we picked up three girls, all in *miliciana* uniform, and then we drove to one of the many army barracks in Cuba that have been converted into schools. Instead of soldiers drilling up and down the parade ground there were now children drilling up and down, and marching off to their classrooms. But of course they were also learning to read and write.

We left the town and headed along the *Carretera Central* to a town called Florida, and then along a dust track to a new co-operative farm.

Suddenly I discovered what the revolution was all about. It put all the ranting and stamping and pistol-packing in their place. This had been part of a rich man's property, but in his time there had been nothing on it except dust and scrub. Now there was a tomato crop growing out of the desert. Wells had been sunk, and water was gushing along mud canals. Yellow tractors were tearing up the remains of the scrub, teams of men were spreading fertilizer over the ploughed land, trucks were bringing loads of empty boxes, and men were picking tomatoes. There were other crops too—cabbages, peppers, rice; and in the middle of the farm a settlement was being built, with rows of little concrete cottages, a school, and a *tienda del pueblo*, a people's shop.

An old Jamaican negro, with little black eyes stitched into his

45

black leather face, was brought along to be introduced. He had come to Cuba forty years ago, when he was sixteen, and had never been back to Jamaica since. Before the revolution he had had casual work in the cane fields and plantations, but no job had ever lasted more than a few months, and he had never known if he would manage to make his savings last until he could find another. Now, for the first time in his life, he had steady employment on the new co-operative.

'I tell people what I think of them,' he said, offering me a special fellow-Britisher friendship. 'If Batista had come along, I'd have told him. If Fidel comes, I'll tell him. He's honest.' And then, to prove he was qualified to judge, he added, 'I can't read Spanish, but I speak it. I read English, though, and I write it too,' and he wrote 'Fidel' on a grubby piece of paper, followed by his own name, 'Jimmy Saunds'.

The white taxi-driver, perhaps to impress the *milicianos*, embraced the old Jamaican, and said, 'We're both Cubans, eh, Jimmy? And there's no colour bar in Cuba, eh, Jimmy?' And old Jimmy said, 'That's right. I'm Jamaican, and I'm Cuban. In Jamaica a black man's not as good as a white man. But in Cuba they're all the same.'

From the co-operative we drove on to a sugar factory, which had lately been owned by an American company but was now state property. Trucks and trains were lining up at the entrance, and pouring their loads of sugar cane into a sunken pit, a tangle of naked brown bamboo. The cane was carried up a belt into a terrifying mashing-machine, chewed first into sticks and then into pulp. Huge steel wheels, so perfectly engineered that they looked almost motionless, gently hummed and flickered, belying their tonnage, and men high up under the roof nonchalantly tripped along the catwalks among the machinery. There was a faint smell of rum. At the far end a final machine was piping pure white castor sugar into paper bags.

Back at the town hall in Camaguey we dropped the three girls and met an old man with grey hair and spectacles, carrying a load of files and notebooks along a passage. In his militia uniform with a pistol and knife in his belt, he looked like a professor dressed up to entertain the children—which was more or less what he was. He talked knowledgeably about Keynes and Marshall and Beveridge, and beamed with pleasure when I told him that his accent was a real English one, with not a trace of American.

'I think England, with its Queen, is more democratic than the United States, with its President. You killed your king once, and one of your kings rebelled against the catholic church, just like us.'

He was too old to fight in the Escambray mountains, but he was proud to have joined the militia, and to have been given a gun. It was made in America: 'All the better to shoot an imperialist with,' he said. 'They kill a *miliciano* every day, so we have to carry arms. We're the ones they're after, because we're really the people, the ordinary people, and we're defending the revolution. We shall win, of course.'

I asked him about the elections that Castro had promised within four years of coming to power. 'Elections? But there's no need of elections. Every time Fidel speaks, he gets his votes. He is not like Hitler. At Hitler's mass meetings the crowd was forced to attend. But in Cuba people go because they want to hear Fidel. And because they love him.' Then he added one of those impressive, unsubstantiated confidences that a traveller in Cuba is always receiving. 'We *know* the American government is paying to help the counter-revolutionaries, and the rebels in the Escambray. We have proof.'

It was Friday evening, and the old professor was on his way to the weekly *charla* organized by the town hall staff, at which a lawyer from Havana was going to speak. He invited me to go along with him.

A *charla* is a debate, but there was no debating here; it was very much a one-man show, and it took place in the headquarters of the town fire brigade. The fire engine had been wheeled out into the street to make room for seats, and all round the walls were hanging oilskins, helmets, boots and axes. A pole disappeared through a hole in the ceiling, and two or three times during the *charla* an astonished fireman slid down it, to find himself in the middle of an audience listening to a talk. Most of the people were elderly women

47

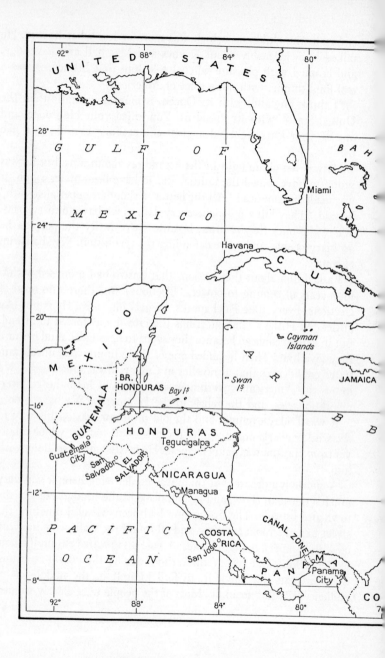

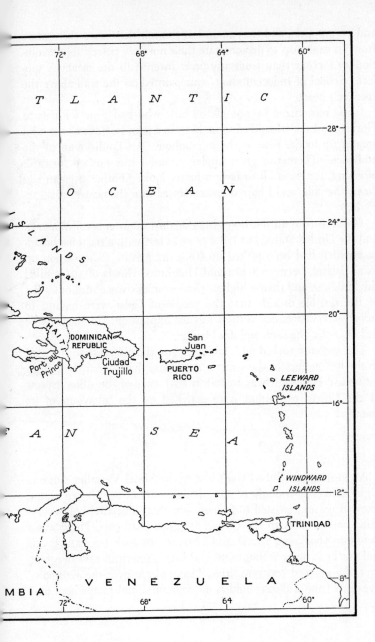

and young girls, and they looked as though they were there more from an eagerness to demonstrate their not very perceptible revolutionary fervour than from any great interest in the speaker's subject. 'School of Indoctrination' was painted on the wall above the speaker's head.

I was recognized by one of the girls who had gone with us to Florida, and she whispered something to a man in front of her who sprang up to the man at the microphone. An Englishman in the audience! There was great applause, and I was pushed forward, blushing, for them all to have a better look. Another fireman slid down the pole, and I bowed and collapsed into the nearest rocking-chair.

The lecture spun on, inveighing against counter-revolutionaries and the United States, but relief came at last with a recorded broadcast which had been picked up from the private radio station on Swan Island, between Cuba and Honduras. Howls of static filled the building, and then a high-pitched woman's voice read out a list of the terrible ordeals that the people of Cuba were having to suffer—starvation, deprivation, torture, oppression. The streets were full of tanks, she said, and dead bodies.

The audience rocked with laughter, and the old professor pointed to the fire-engines in the street: 'I suppose that's what they mean by tanks.' Perhaps it was a comfort that some of the sillier aspects of the Cuban revolution were matched by the behaviour of its enemies.

*　　　*　　　*

At Santiago de Cuba I went first to the Motel Versalles, but one night there was enough. It was a little corner of the United States, screwed up and twisted to fit a society that, officially, held everything connected with the United States as anathema. There was a swimming-pool, and a view, and a breeze, and little trees and lawns and cracked concrete fountains, and huge American cars sweeping over the cracked concrete drive. 'Somewhere over the Rainbow' streamed from a dozen hidden microphones, and somewhere over

50

the ocean the Cubans who might have enjoyed it were enjoying the real thing, in Florida and California.

To give it a country club atmosphere, the bedrooms were built of bare brick and furnished with pine cupboards and string-and-basket chairs, but everything was warped and peeling. There was a shop near the reception desk that sold folksy souvenirs, and in the empty dining-room a party of Cubans sat alone while one of their women sang songs from old films about Texas and Naples in a devastating wobbly voice. A drunkard at the bar, imitating the woman, set up dreadful falsetto howls, like some unknown monster baying at the moon, and the waiters dutifully laughed. Two sad Czechs asked me hopefully if I was Swedish, and looked even sadder when they learnt I wasn't.

I fled to the Casa Grande, an old hotel in the main square next to the cathedral. From my window, beyond a rubbish dump and a dentist's sign, I could see the Union Jack flying over the British consulate. 'It's a hot-bed of revolution,' said the vice-consul, 'and all the bedrooms are wired for sound.' Certainly there were always crowds of men and women in militia uniform hanging around the veranda, and one evening I found myself caught up in a reception for a catholic priest who had condemned his own church for imperialism and had immediately been gathered up by the revolution and toted round Cuba as a hero.

On Sunday a crowd of young men who had been lounging outside the cathedral slipped in just as mass was beginning and sat down at the back. The nave was almost full, with people of all ages and colours, but nobody in uniform. Afterwards, a brass band set itself up in the square—uniforms and sousaphones and all—and played a marvellously vulgar trumpet concerto while the population paraded under the floodlamps hanging from the trees. 'Paredón for the priests, the lacqueys of Yankee imperialism!' was illuminated on the front of the town hall; and a big car standing underneath it had a sticker in its back window: 'We are catholics. In case of an accident, please call a priest."

There seemed to be more animation in Santiago than in Havana, and a more genuine Cuban flavour; more genuine poverty, too.

51

Trying to find the port one hot afternoon, I found myself walking down a steep narrow street of steps and cobbles. Behind me came the clip-clip of high heels, and a most provocative mulatto girl in tight cotton trousers overtook me. As she passed me she began to count in English, pretending that it was the most natural thing in the world: 'One, two, three, four, five . . .' and walked on. A few yards ahead of me she stopped, bent down in her tight trousers and pulled up her sock; then, when I had caught her up again, she walked on beside me, still counting, 'Thirteen, fourteen, sixteen,' (she wasn't very good). Walking faster than me, she again stopped ahead, bent down and waited till I had caught her up: 'Twenty-four, twenty-five.' But after I had walked past her a second time, ignoring her, she gave up the game.

Further down the street I came to more girls, sitting behind the doors of their houses and looking out through open panels that revealed their heads and shoulders and the top half of their bosoms. Dignified and beautiful they looked, waiting for their customers—sailors up from the docks, or Cubans down from the town.

*   *   *

As I was sitting in a café having breakfast a ragged beggar boy came in and slunk round the room, picking his nose with a filthy finger and kicking the wall. He came up to my table, kicked a chair and silently stared at the coffee pot. I was enjoying my coffee and the sun slanting on to the table, and he spoilt it all. Selfishly I didn't want to be bothered with him.

The smartest woman in the café, sitting at a table with her own little boy, who had a fine blue suit and polished shoes, called the beggar over and asked him to sit with them. She ordered more coffee for him, and when it came she put sugar and a pinch of salt into it. The beggar boy didn't say a word, and the woman didn't once look at me.

*   *   *

One morning before dawn a motor torpedo-boat slid into Santiago harbour and opened fire on the nationalized oil refinery. A watchman was killed and small fires were started, before the boat turned round and sailed out of the harbour, undamaged and unidentified.

To an outsider it seemed a most dashing adventure, in the best Caribbean tradition, but Castro in a speech next day, claiming that the torpedo boat came either from the American naval base at Guantánamo along the coast or from Jamaica, described it as another shameful example of imperialist cowardice. All the newspapers printed pages of photographs of the dead watchman and his mourning wife, and any curiosity as to how a pirate could penetrate without any opposition into Santiago harbour, the entrance of which is less than two hundred yards wide and several miles long, was smothered by a demand for the nation's sympathy for a family bereft of a heroic revolutionary.

A few evenings later a mammoth demonstration was staged in the cathedral square, to protest against the attack. It began with a crocodile of schoolgirls in school uniform marching into the square chanting in their high-pitched voices, 'Paredón for the priests, paredón for the priests!' thus increasing the confusion by adding an alternative slogan. They lined up opposite the town hall where a small pulpit had been erected—I thought at first it was a scaffold—and where loudspeakers were being strung from the trees and lamp posts. More contingents arrived—one of dock workers, another from the Federation of Cuban Women, another from the oil refinery that had suffered the brutal, cowardly attack—all carrying banners and singing slogans, and supported by two brass bands.

One of the bands set itself up in the portico of the town hall and began to play whatever came into its head, which was usually the tune that was being sung by the people standing closest to it. More and more people streamed in, and very soon the town hall end of the square was packed full, while at the other end, near the cathedral, everything was as calm as ever, with men and women sitting on benches under the trees, chatting, dreaming, buying oranges or watching the children play. A platoon of milicianas, the plainest lot of women I've ever seen, took up a position behind the pulpit and

53

plunged into a wild chant that spread through the crowd like an infection, and for a few minutes a kind of awful unison was achieved, before rival squads started up other slogans.

Among the earnest *milicianos* round the pulpit there was a desperate anxiety to inject a little discipline into the meeting, but for the majority it was just a happy night out, with a lot of community singing; there was no dignity and very little common purpose, but simply a few dozen groups of happy, hysterical youths, each trying to shout louder than the next.

The band in the portico seemed in a constant quandary, the tubas playing one tune and the clarinets another, until all the players were seized with a sudden single-mindedness and charged into the March of the Twenty-Sixth of July. 'Marching! We are marching to an ideal!' The entire crowd dropped their individual slogans and joined in. 'At the altars of peace and prosperity we shall triumph! We shall fight everyone for our freedom!' It was an impressive noise, three or four thousand people singing in a cathedral square. 'Forward, Cubans! Our heroism will be rewarded!'

When it was over, a man climbed up into the pulpit and began yelling into a microphone, but the crowd were not ready for speeches yet; they wanted to go on shouting. Anyway, the loudspeakers had been erected on the opposite side of the road and were facing away from most of the people and towards the cathedral, so that the shouters in front, who were the noisiest, couldn't hear what was being said to them. The shouts and chants filled the crowded half of the square, and the man's voice filled the empty, calm half. Very soon he gave up.

Ten minutes later the band plunged into the March of the Twenty-Sixth of July again. 'We shall purge Cuba with fire, until the end of this infernal plague of detestable governments and insatiable tyrants who have plunged it into misery! Never shall we forget the blood which flowed in Cuba!' Before the last chord had ended the man at the microphone began his tirade.

But still the crowd was not ready, and with an ear-splitting scream from somewhere, '*Cuba Sí, Yankees No!*' they were off again on their slogans. It wasn't till the band had played the March for a third time that the crowd was finally controlled. A fox-faced *miliciano*, a man with incredible hatred in his eyes, yelled something down the microphone and there was a momentary hush. In a voice thick with an artificial throb he called for a minute's silence in memory of the dead revolutionary, stepped back from the microphone and bowed his head. There were tremendous shushing noises through the square, and at last silence. Then the speeches began.

The parade took on the air of a religious service attended by a congregation of high-spirited but irreverent children. They paid very little attention to the speeches from the pulpit, chattering and laughing and starting up little slogan-chanting competitions among themselves. But all the time they kept an ear cocked for the speaker as he screamed his way through the liturgy, and when he came to the well-known passages, the familiar words of hate and adoration, they all joined in with the correct responses. Talking in church was allowed, so long as the congregation came in at the right places.

Somebody nudged my arm. '*Sprechen Sie Deutsch?*' It was a little grey-haired man, mild and smiling. 'Ah, sir, then we can talk in English. Yes, sir, it is great pleasure, sir. I am Hungarian. Yes, sir, half Hungarian and half Viennese. Yes, sir, thirty-six years now I have been in Cuba. I didn't like it in Hungary then, sir, so I came to Cuba. When I came, I was musician. Yes, sir, violinist. I was leader of the Havana symphony orchestra. Then I came to Santiago. Now I am professor. I teach English and commerce, sir. Oh yes, sir, it is much better now in Cuba. The people, you see, are much happier. Oh yes, sir. Just look. They are so happy. And they enjoy it. They love their revolution. Are you a revolutionary, sir? I think all Englishmen are revolutionaries. Yes, sir. Even the King. Yes, sir, I think so. I thought you were Russian, and then I spoke in German, but you are English. I can speak Russian a little. Look, sir, I will write it in Russian for you—"Fatherland or Death, we shall win!" There, sir.'

The crowd had started singing a patriotic song, and the band joined in, but in another key. The second band at the far end of the town hall also started on the same tune, in the same key but at a slower speed, so that every few bars it had to skip a note or two to catch up.

'You see, sir, they are so happy. And I am happy too, to meet you. Yes, sir. Good luck to you sir, and good luck to the King of England, sir. Thank you sir."

With so much screaming around me, and the horrible man in the pulpit, and all the gruesome slogans held up on banners, I wondered vaguely if I was being rather brave, a solitary imperialist standing in the middle of so much hate. But most of the people were not really hating; they were just a lot of silly youths without a thought in their heads beyond a momentary desire to scream louder than anybody else. It was fun, too, to clap one's hands in unison to the rhythm of ' *Paredón* for the priests ! ' and even more fun when the chant turned into a Cuban rumba. What did terrify me, however, was the sight of an elderly woman in khaki uniform, with a pistol in her belt and a faint moustache on her lip, yelling for the blood of the priests, her great breasts heaving up and down as she stamped and clapped.

At the other end of the square the doors of the great cathedral, built only thirty years after Columbus' first voyage, stood open, and inside people were sitting in the pews or praying. Except for the blast of the loudspeakers, all was peace; a deaf man wouldn't have noticed anything unusual.

*   *   *

I sat for three hours in the Santiago office of INRA, the National Institute for Agrarian Reform, waiting to see the provincial director. Pretty girls clacked around on their stiletto heels, in contrast to the men, who were almost all in uniform. For the headquarters of an organization in charge of such a peaceful job there seemed to be an unnecessary amount of pistols and carbines and knives about. Some of the men were swashbuckling, and carried their weapons with panache and confidence, but others seemed pulled down by the weight of so much armoury. There was an atmosphere of profound inefficiency, coupled with a bonhomie that would be rare in a government office in most other countries.

Eventually I was led in to meet the director, a most impressive man with a beard and a twinkle, and, it seemed, a colossal capacity for work. He was a doctor and had worked for the United Nations in Germany after the war; during the three minutes in which I sat opposite him, he dictated a letter, spoke to an INRA branch at the other end of the province over the radio and dealt with me. He was a man with inspiration and energy, alone among a lot of idlers kicking their table legs, talking to their friends on the telephone, drinking coffee and Coca-Cola. Cuba is run by such people, the handful of visionaries presiding over a welter of subordinates who support the government with more noise than usefulness. With a laugh, he offered me a jeep and a driver, Miguel, and a three-day tour of Oriente Province.

In a Santiago suburb Miguel showed me the remains of a shanty slum that was being torn down; a few hovels of tin and wood patch-work still stood among the wreckage. The desolation and misery of those hutches were so extreme that, even though I knew they were people's homes, they seemed irrelevant and incomprehensible. Even the inhabitants, standing in the mud with pale unsmiling faces and ragged bodies, scarcely touched me, so far were they from any human experience. The shock didn't reach me until, a few hundred yards away, Miguel showed me an estate of newly built bungalows, dreadful in their pastel shades and flimsy, vulgar uniformity, but at least connected visibly with life.

From there we went to a farm just outside the city, where pigs and cattle were being reared on land that had previously been part of a rich man's estate, but which had never been properly worked. New buildings and fences and roads had appeared, and, most important of all, the local peasants were now employed.

It was the same story at another, bigger farm, that was being managed by an old veteran who had fought with Castro in the mountains of the Sierra Maestra. He had once been a small-time capitalist, with a factory of his own and enough money to spend his holidays in the United States, but having once buckled on his pistol

57

and grown a beard, he had surrendered happily to the revolution. The previous landowner, who had been a senator in Batista's government but had only employed about a dozen men to look after the few cows that roamed the hills, was now in Miami, and would never be allowed back. The new owners, said the manager, would drive him off the land if he ever dared return. They had changed the whole farm, with tomatoes, sugar cane, onions, maize, piggeries and cowsheds. The barns were stacked with sacks of beans and cotton, and the peasants had even built a new town, rows and rows of little houses painted pink or yellow or blue, standing in their own little gardens and glowing, as it were, at the thought of free electricity, free water and free rent. There was a *tienda del pueblo*, and a school, complete with its own Martí Corner, where the Apostle's whitewashed head brooded dejectedly between two little vases of flowers. But there was no church.

Men rode about the farm on horses, wearing cowboy hats and carrying guns, and silently admiring the big American tractors ploughing up the land. In the face of work like this, the shortage of soap in the towns, of milk bottles and babies' nappies and corn flakes, didn't really matter.

There was one thing on the farm, however, which the manager didn't want to talk about: rows of roofless houses waiting for timber, with their concrete walls already cracking, the ends of the steel reinforcement bars rusting, and weeds growing up inside. Perhaps somebody's enthusiasm had been greater than the supply of raw materials. The manager quickly changed the subject, and over a jug of iced coconut milk he delivered a tirade in a strong Texan accent about the need to defend Cuba against the imperialists; the peasants knew at last what it felt like to own and work their land, and they would never give it up. Besides, the land had never been worked so well.

'But I don't think we have any trouble from England. Though we get plenty trouble from the States. Boy!'

Miguel and I drove west to Manzanillo, stopping on the way at the huge school-city that was being built in the foothills of the Sierra Maestra. Twenty thousand children would eventually live in its

58

gaily-coloured buildings scattered over the hillside, facing across to the mountains where their homes were and where their Fidel fought.

The earnest, dedicated headmaster began to show me round, but suddenly he was called away to receive a delegation from the Institute for Friendship with the Peoples. A squadron of Cadillacs swept up the drive, and out stepped the visitors—an Italian, three Chinese and a representative from almost every country in Latin America. There was also an Australian dressed up in Cuban army uniform who slapped me on the back, called me a ' Pommie bastard ', and said he had arrived recently in Cuba to help defend it against the imperialists; the promised invasion had never turned up, but he was staying on in the army until he had learnt enough Spanish to qualify for a proper role in the revolution. Several months later I met him again in Havana; he had become a cartoonist on the communist daily paper, *Hoy*.

Somehow—possibly by exercising my three or four words of Mandarin on the Chinese, who clapped their hands and said, ' Very revolutionary, very revolutionary '—I got swept up into the delegation, and was treated to a tour of the school-city and a lecture and a feast that were usually only granted to proper Friendly Peoples. We trailed from class-rooms to playing-fields to dining-rooms, took photographs of children having lunch and playing basketball, and behaved towards each other with a mixture of forced conviviality and suspicion. The Australian went on slapping backs and pouring out a stream of praise in a language of his own, half Spanish of a kind, and half Sydney slang of quite another kind; and the three Chinese went on clapping and saying, ' Very revolutionary, very revolutionary ' about everything they were shown, from the television set in one of the class-rooms to the spaghetti and beer we were given for lunch. But they all treated me as hopelessly untouchable, quite unqualified for membership of their friendship club.

Miguel and I escaped from the delegation and drove down the coast to the place where Castro landed in December 1956. With eighty-one men and a lot of arms crammed into a motor launch called *Granma* he had crossed over from Mexico where they had been training, and made a landfall at about the most forbidding stretch of Cuban coast they could have found. They first had to hack their way through a mile of mangrove swamps, wading and floundering with their equipment, and then it was a long march up into the Sierra Maestra. Within a few weeks the party was reduced by death and desertion to twelve, but two years later Castro rode in triumph down the island to Havana. Those twelve men had conquered the country.

Now there was a wooden cat-walk a mile long through the mangroves to the point where the *Granma* landed, and a notice at the end: 'Here was born the freedom of Cuba, December 12, 1956.' We sat on a fallen tree and Miguel pulled out his revolver and started potting at mangrove stumps. Suddenly, down the cat-walk, came tripping the delegation, covered in dust but still irrepressibly enthusiastic. The Australian seized another pistol and began firing wildly into the sea, and the three Chinese, startled at the noise of so much gunfire, stood with their fingers in their ears, whimpering quietly, 'Very revolutionary.'

That evening at Manzanillo we met them all again. At sunset I walked down to the shore and stood with the sea lapping smellily at my feet, watching a family of pelicans sitting on a row of posts in the water; and the pelicans watched me. As the sun sank behind a string of islands on the horizon the pelicans left their perches and began to fish. They toppled and splashed into the water, flapped heavily up again, toppled and splashed again, but with a kind of ridiculous elegance quite out of character with their cumbersome and costive appearance.

'Very revolutionary,' said a voice behind me. 'Very revolutionary.'

*   *   *

'OPERATION FAMILY
Collaborate with the Ministry of Justice
in Operation Family!
Utilize the benefits of Law 797!
Co-operate with Collective Marriages!'

It was a startling notice to see in a café in Pinar del Río, but it didn't mean what I thought. It was simply an advertisement for the mass civil weddings organized by a puritan government for couples who had been happily living together for years, and attended, presumably, by all the children.

*   *   *

It was easy enough to meet counter-revolutionaries. In fact, they often seemed more voluble than revolutionaries, but they were usually people who had a personal grudge—a requisitioned house or an expropriated farm—and who latched on to the first person who might be willing to listen to their moans. Better still if that person was a foreigner on whom they could practise their English.

I wanted to meet someone belonging to an organized opposition who could tell me more about the counter-revolution than just a hard-luck story. I made careful inquiries in Santiago de Cuba, and one night I was taken in a taxi to a villa in a residential suburb and introduced to a man of about thirty-five, a civil engineer, who told me that he was in touch with all counter-revolutionary movements both in Cuba and in Miami, and could tell me anything I wanted to know.

I asked him, first of all, why it was that anybody, apart from the dispossessed landowners and capitalists, should be discontented with the government. Why, for instance, should the ordinary peasant be anything but pleased with the new order?

The peasant, said the engineer, was exactly the man who had suffered most under the new government. In his little *bohío*, with his patch of maize, a couple of pigs, a cow, a few chickens and a woman or two, he had been master of his destiny. Perhaps he had worked on a rich man's estate, or in the local sugar factory, but he had always had his own little plot, and though terribly poor he had been able to indulge in his three favourite pleasures—rum, cockfighting and women.

But now almost every peasant had been herded into a co-operative, and given a new house, smaller than his old *bohío*, to which he

61

hadn't even been allowed to bring his animals. His pigs had been put in a communal piggery, half his wages came in the form of tickets which could only be spent at the *tienda del pueblo*, and he had been bullied into marrying one of his women.

To me this sounded like the old coal-in-the-bath story. Even peasants are adaptable, and nobody really minds moving from a leaky, ramshackle hut into a pale-blue, flat-roofed concrete house, even if it is exactly like the pale green one next door. In the context of backward countries like Cuba, old-fashioned cant about the private individual crumbles in the face of purely material improvement. Cubans, say the counter-revolutionaries, are individuals at heart; but who in the world, I wonder, is not an individual at heart —except when it comes to a choice between abject squalor and comparative luxury.

All that the peasants needed, said the engineer, was a gun. Give them a gun and they'd rise up tomorrow. I pointed out that thousands of them who had joined the militia already had guns, but that they didn't seem to me to be on the point of revolt; to which the engineer glibly replied that the militia itself was one of the most vehement counter-revolutionary forces, and was just waiting for a suitable chance to declare itself.

Perhaps because I seemed so sceptical he offered to show me how extensive the counter-revolution was, and how well organized. Up in the mountains of Oriente Province, he said, there were two thousand men being trained to fight and being supplied with funds and weapons from Miami. He knew a man who could arrange for me to visit them, and he asked me, if I agreed to go, whether I would do my best to help them. Would I write something that would bring them publicity and encouragement? Would I tell Latin America what was being done to cut out the communist cancer? Would I tell the world? Suddenly a suspicion crossed his mind. Was I sympathetic? Was I anti-Castro? Had I got any references?

But he didn't really doubt that all Englishmen were like the Americans, and firmly anti-Castro. He said that I must be ready to start tomorrow. The trip might last a week, or it might be possible to do it in a day; he didn't know. I might have to cut my hair short, and wear a big straw hat. A day in the sun, he was sure, would burn my face to a more Cuban colour. Could they be sure I wasn't a spy? Well, it would be up to the other man. The fighters were scattered all over the mountains, so I should not be able to see more than two or three isolated groups; but there were two thousand in Oriente Province alone, and thousands more in the rest of Cuba. I was not to be too surprised if the jeep that took me on the first part of the journey was an INRA one, or an army one, for the government and even the G-2, the secret police, were deep in the counter-revolution. How many days' walking in the jungle did I think my shoes would stand? Five or six? Very well, then, tomorrow evening he would come to the Casa Grande and let me know what had been arranged. We shook hands on it.

He never came the next day, nor the day after. As I sat waiting for him on the veranda overlooking the cathedral square I began to remember other things he had told me. He had been the engineer in charge of building a road across the mountains, but had lost the job when the workers had demonstrated outside his office, clamouring for some of the things that Castro had promised them in a speech when he visited them. Another man, who was not an engineer at all, had been appointed in his place—one of those insidious people who were beginning to appear in universities, schools, hospitals and ministries to keep an eye on the professionals, guide the institution in the proper direction, and make spectacular demonstrations to the public. Then I remembered another thing he had said : 'I am an American addict,' and I began to curse myself for having believed so much of what he had told me.

*   *   *

'On my way back from my trip to Russia and China,' said a Cuban poet, 'I stopped in Poland, and there I ate strawberries and strawberries and strawberries, because I thought we should never have them again in Cuba. But when I got back here I found that we had started to grow them ourselves. They are marvellous, perfectly *marvellous*.'

We had just had lunch at the *Gato Tuerto* and he was going home.

'This afternoon,' he said, 'I think I shall write a poem about love. I work for the revolution, but I simply can't write poetry about tractors, as they do in China.'

* * *

I arrived by bus one hot afternoon at Sancti Spiritus and stood in the main square miserably bleating, 'Trinidad, Trinidad,' which was the name of the town I wanted to reach that night. A fat young man with thick eyebrows and a mighty stomach, who was sitting up in a wooden armchair having his cowboy boots polished, told me that there was no bus to Trinidad before five o'clock next morning, and that as the road was under military control no taxis were allowed down it; it ran along the foot of the Escambray mountains, where there was a campaign being fought against the *gusanos*, the grubs. Anyway, he added, I would need a military pass.

He was so pessimistic that I resigned myself to waiting for the early morning bus and took a room in a hotel; but the room was even more discouraging, and I went back to bleating in the square. The fat young man stepped down from his throne, and putting on a huge cowboy hat flicked his fingers and jerked his chin towards an empty jeep standing across the road. Fecklessly I got in and he started up; we drove like madmen, scattering people and animals and leaving them spluttering in our dust, to a military headquarters two or three miles out of town, where the cowboy sat silently chewing in his jeep while I asked for a pass to Trinidad.

I had with me a letter from the government newspaper, *Revolución*, addressed to revolutionary functionaries and authorities, introducing me as a señor Englishman who found himself disposed to make a journey through Cuba; in view of the importance that the journey could have in helping to counteract the campaign of calumnies against Cuba which the imperialist press was waging abroad, the letter asked all authorities and functionaries of the
64

revolutionary government, members of the rebel army of the militias and all revolutionary Cubans with whom the señor established contact, to give him the greatest help and co-operation for the happy unfolding of his journalistic and informative work; it ended up, ' *Patria o Muerte!* ' and worked like magic.

I was given a pass and got back into the jeep. The cowboy kicked the clutch, the jeep snorted, and away we sped. Ten minutes later he dropped me at a bridge a couple of miles down the road to Trinidad, and with a crunch of dust and gravel and a flourish of his hat he wheeled round and charged back to the town. I found myself standing in the sun with a *miliciano* sentry.

Soon a car came along and was stopped by the *miliciano*, but it was full and there was no room for me; then another came, but it wasn't going as far as Trinidad. The third car was a huge Ford which seemed to be quite empty as it approached the bridge, but when it stopped I saw a tiny man in army officer's uniform, a lieutenant, sitting on the front seat behind the wheel. Although he wasn't going to Trinidad he insisted on taking me as far as an army camp about ten miles on, where I could certainly get another lift. I got in, and within a few hundred yards we were doing eighty; the lieutenant could only just touch the pedals, even with his high-heeled riding boots.

With gestures that would have been expansive on a man three times his size, he talked about the bitter fighting that was going on in the mountains and about the bravery of the *milicianos* and the contemptibility of the grubs; but there were only a few hundred of them left, he said, raising himself to spit out of the window, and it would all be over in a few days.

The camp was like a holiday camp that had been invaded by a crowd of irresponsible boy scouts. Hundreds of young *milicianos* were mooching around, drinking beer in the canteen, singing and having their photos taken by a civilian photographer who was posing them in ferocious attitudes, with rifles brandished above their heads and their youthful beards stuck out at a properly menacing angle. But though they were all smothered with weapons they looked about as dangerous as a gang of kids playing cowboys and Indians. They wore necklaces of dried nuts, and crucifixes, and they had decorated their uniforms with badges, ribbons and feathers.

The midget lieutenant tripped through the camp on his high heels and led me into a little room where he introduced me to his wife. Then he called for beer, and for Rosita. She arrived, a plump girl about twice his size, with huge placid eyes and an air of utter lifelessness. The lieutenant clutched her by the hips and twisted her round to show me her back and her great bottom. Was there anything so pretty in the whole of England? Of course not! Long live the revolution!

After three bottles of beer I said I really must be going, and the lieutenant pressed me to another beer, and then another. Finally he said that there was absolutely no hope of a lift on to Trinidad that evening, so he would take me there himself. We got back into the car, and four *milicianos*, with their rifles and knives and ammunition pouches, got in with us. They had all been at the camp for exactly seventy-six days and had never yet left it, let alone been up in the mountains to fight the grubs. Helped on by the beer the lieutenant drove even faster than before, which made the *milicianos* glow with happiness and patriotic pride.

Fortunately the beer, or boredom, overcame the lieutenant, and recognizing two militia officers in a car which he passed at a terrifying speed he stopped, waited for them to catch up, and asked them if they could take me to Trinidad. They too were only going to another camp a few miles on, but were willing to take me there. Thankfully I watched the lieutenant with his *milicianos* roar back to their beer and Rosita.

The next camp was as full of idle *milicianos* as the first, drinking beer and coffee, smoking cigars and endlessly hitching their rifles up on their shoulders. The comforting knowledge that their employers back home were still having to pay their wages, and that the attention of the whole nation was being persistently drawn to their gallantry, didn't relieve the terrible tedium of soldiering in a campaign that entailed no action whatever.

I was asked for my pass, and then ignored for so long that I began to despair of getting away that night. A group of officers came to the door of a hut and one of them pointed at me, and then they went back in again. Finally one of the bearded officers who had brought me came out and said that he had decided to go home to Cienfuegos for the night and would drop me off in Trinidad on the way through.

The road to Trinidad ran between the sea and the mountains, and there were *milicianos* all the way. They were living in miserable bivouacs in the undergrowth by the roadside, or in leaf huts that they had made for themselves, or just in the rain; as we drove past, some of them came running on to the road waving plates and kettles, in the hope that we might be the daily kitchen truck with its oil drum full of stew.

I asked the officer what they were all doing, when it had been announced weeks earlier that the Escambray campaign had been finished, and he replied that there were still a few grubs up in the mountains who had to be exterminated. Then, to stall my remonstration that surely so many thousands of young men were not needed for only a handful of grubs, he added that there were other reasons for keeping them in the Escambray. They were being trained, and taught discipline and the rudiments of mountain warfare; most important, they were there for the good of the local peasants, to educate them, help them build proper houses, teach them about good farming, clean living and the revolution. He hinted that, because the peasants in the mountains had been so insulated both by the difficult country and their own backwardness from the benefits of the revolution, they had not been as hostile to the grubs who had taken refuge in the Escambray as they might have been. They had to be taught to be good revolutionaries.

But enough of that. 'What do they say about our revolution in England?'

When we reached Trinidad it was almost dark.

'You can't possibly stay here! It's too old-fashioned. Look, cobbles, cobbles, nothing but cobbles! It's filthy. No decent hotel. You'd better come on to Cienfuegos.' Trinidad, where Cortés prepared his expedition for the conquest of Mexico, I had imagined to be a pretty Spanish colonial town with sleepy squares and big baroque churches—and perhaps it was. But it was too easy to be persuaded to continue to Cienfuegos, and we drove on into the night.

'Do you like crabs?' asked the officer suddenly. Ahead on the road I saw what looked like leaves fluttering on the tarmac, being blown from one verge to the other; but there were no trees near. We reached the first leaf, and it was a huge crab. Further on, the road was almost completely covered with them—black crabs, pink crabs, white crabs, yellow crabs; crabs of every size. There was more crab than road. It was like a swarm of ants, but the ants had grown into crabs, and they extended for five miles. They were coming up from the scrub between the sea and the road, creeping through the bivouacs of the *milicianos*, and crossing over into the grass on the other side. What they were planning to do in the grass I don't know, but many of them never got there. The officer tried to avoid killing them, and as we approached they scuttled hysterically backwards and forwards and then stopped petrified in front of us, their little black pin-eyes starting from their shells and their clippers waving pathetically for mercy. Hundreds of them had been crushed by army lorries, and remained hobbling with a leg hanging off, or lay squashed out of existence for the luckier ones to feast off. However much he zigzagged the officer only contributed to the slaughter, as the tyres crunched through crab shells and spattered crab-meat up on to the car; the smell of crab-meat roasting on the exhaust pipe hung with us all the way to Cienfuegos.

*   *   *

Through the sugar fields, pulling huge wooden carts stacked with cane and crackling over the fallen stalks, lumbered the ox teams; and little trains, rocking and whistling, rattled along the narrow tracks to the factory—toy trains, but looking more like real trains than real trains ever do. The slender factory chimney erect with its banner of black smoke waving over the country was freshly painted, 'We shall conquer!' and around the sidings and lorries and wagons drifted a faint smell of rum.

Volunteer parties went out from the towns at weekends to cut cane, and Castro and the Chinese ambassador went with them, and were photographed slaking their thirst from the same tin mug. Beyond the cane fields were green meadows, where cows placidly flicked their tails at flies as they grazed against a frieze of palm trees.

In Pinar del Río province, at the western end of Cuba, I went to a cotton co-operative, and a fishery co-operative, and a tobacco co-operative. At the first I was shouted at by workers picking cotton in the sun to go and join them, and invited by one of them into his brand new house. On a bare brick wall he had the regulation portrait of the *Máximo Líder*, and on the opposite wall a slightly less regulation print of the Last Supper, and in the kitchen he had a highly un-regulation peasant's wife, with painted toenails and a delicious tendency to say, 'Oh, brother!'—though it was the only English she knew.

Through the window she pointed to the rows of other new bungalows, all painted in dainty pastel shades, and the new school, and the new social welfare centre, and the new canteen, and the new *tienda del pueblo*. But there was no new church. 'Oh, brother!' We went into the *tienda del pueblo* and she picked up a tin of Russian beef and a tin of Japanese sardines. 'Oh, brother!'

At the fishermen's co-operative I saw twenty new fishing-boats being built in a shed, and had a marvellous meal of crab and rice and beer in a state-owned restaurant crammed with happy, noisy, ebullient holiday-makers, while far out to sea the breakers crashing on the reef flashed snow-white in the sun.

The tobacco co-operative was a model show-piece, and named after two young brothers killed during the Batista regime. Walking down the rows of tobacco plants I marvelled at the care, skill, labour and money being spent on a crop that is eaten by nobody. A tremendous rainstorm had just passed, hosing on to the fields and squeezing all the rich flavour from the wet, red soil. The great leaves dripped heavily on to each other, and in the sun the air smelt almost surprisingly of fresh tobacco. One field was in flower, and again

69

surprisingly the flower was the same little white trumpet with the marvellous sweet scent of June evenings in an English garden. All across the country were wooden barns, like the towerless naves of Gothic cathedrals, steep-roofed and filled with tobacco leaves hung for curing.

* * *

'*Paredón! Paredón!*' screamed the mob, with the same terrifying hysteria that drove another mob, in another land, to yell, 'Crucify him!' But life was cheap in Latin America—or so they said—and the Cubans were well accustomed to blood.

There were other things which they were not accustomed to. Cuba is a tropical country, with the kind of society that the tropics breed—inclined to laziness, and contented with the minimum. They had been used, if not to a high standard of living, at least to having it around them—to a vision of wealth and luxury not seen in other countries struck by communism except by a tiny aristocracy. They may have been only too well acquainted with poverty, but austerity and thrift were words unknown. The climate was kind and the land was fertile, and with a little exertion a man could make enough money for another cigar.

In a few years that vision of wealth disappeared and the foundations of society, rotten and decayed as they were, crumbled. A substitute was presented, but beyond the superficial appeal to the emotions of a passionate, nationalistic people and the excitement aroused by campaigns such as the attack on the church, the war against the counter-revolution and the organized hatred of the United States—beyond the particular demonstration of the moment, whose attraction was merely the fun of the fair—the new order commanded more bewilderment and erratic enthusiasm than unity or a sense of purpose. It was nice to be in the news, and to be watched by the world, but it must have been disheartening to be reminded, by the fumbling inefficiency of government departments, by the shortages in the shops, by the abuses perpetrated in the name of that omnipotent divinity 'the people', and by the denial of

70

any right to criticize, that all was not as well as it might be. And offers of eternal friendship from the people of Outer Mongolia were cold comfort.

With a chronic shortage of foreign exchange, of drugs and machinery, of experienced administrators and technicians, Cuba was in an unenviable state. The revolutionary leaders may have been selfless and dedicated, but with a huge vacuum of bureaucratic inefficiency beneath them, at the level where jobs require competence rather than inspiration, they were all too liable to be tossed hither and thither by the very much cleverer men of Moscow and Peking. And the people, so far from falling in step behind the banners of socialism, progress and liberty, merely felt baffled and bemused. Despite its boasts it was not a revolution of the peasants and workers; it was a revolution of the middle class, and its sharpest irony was that it contrived to destroy the middle class.

These were thoughts that nagged at me after two months in Cuba. There was a feeling of instability—not a back-to-the-wall desperation, but an admission that the counter-revolution, though in a worse muddle than the revolution, nevertheless threatened. This uneasiness could be seen in the quantity of militia men and women everywhere, in the guns and uniforms, in the appeals for patriotism and the demonstrations. It was in the apoplectic attitude towards the United States, and in the venomous campaign towards the priests; it was in the disaffection among the traditional rebels, the students and intellectuals, and in the purges of the universities; it was in the hesitancy and deceit and arbitrary, almost fickle, behaviour of the officials I met. This revolution was fluid; it was still revolving.

Castro made his five-hour speeches, juggling with every slogan and twisting each point a dozen ways and rubbing it in until it hurt; as repetitive and monotonous as Cuban music—the mumbo-jumbo of the mamba-rumba. It was comforting never to be troubled by hecklers, not to be obliged to answer questions or argue. The only interruptions were for applause—' Fi-DEL!' or ' Cuba sí, Yankees no!'—and when the shouting went on too long somebody only had to switch on the National Anthem to restore order. Next morning

71

the papers were full of big close-up shots of the *Máximo Líder*, nervously adjusting the microphones and much moved.

The fact that twelve men on their own in the mountains had brought seven million Cubans to their feet, showed not only what sort of men those twelve were, but also what sort the seven million were. If people get the government they deserve, the Cubans deserved both Batista and Castro. But the longer I stayed in Cuba the more I felt that they deserved something altogether different from the tragedy that seemed to lie ahead—whether it was a civil war or just an increasingly unsteady economy and an increasingly tyrannous rule. I had come to Cuba with hopes of finding something exciting, dynamic and romantic. What I found seemed more like the despotism of a megalomaniac demagogue, and the apathy of a misguided population. Compared with the past, which is the best judgement, it was good; but compared with what it might have been it was tragic. It had turned sour. The Cuban people had done nothing to deserve that. The Cuban people, in fact, had done nothing at all.

*   *   *

'Hey, feller! Where you been?' A fat man with a face that glowed with unbelievable salacity, held out his hand, clapped me on the shoulder, and sat down beside me. 'Where you been?' he repeated, before I had time to remember where we had met before. Then I remembered that we had never met before.

He suddenly noticed my camera. 'Hey, feller! You know where the best pictures are?'

The best pictures? He must mean pornographic ones, and I tried to think of the name of a night club, any night club.

'Hey feller! You know where you get the best pictures?'

I longed to know, but I was English and confused, and I couldn't guess.

'Hey, feller! In the jail-house.'

*   *   *

Cuba, lying in the middle of the Caribbean, topographically like a large caterpillar but politically more like a Colorado beetle, may be a paradox, but certainly it is composed of millions of smaller paradoxes. It is a weird, effervescent mixture of blood and Coca-Cola, of violence and indolence, apathy and passion.

In the state-owned supermarkets of Havana there were tins of Russian meat and fish for sale, and bottles of Scotch whisky and Spanish wine. There was an amusement park called Coney Island, and a cinema called the Patrice Lumumba. My neighbour on the right in a bar said that the government would fall in six months, and my neighbour on the left that the country was behind Castro to a man. One said that the rebels in the Escambray were a real counter-revolution, supplied by Cubans in exile in Miami with the support of the United States; the other said that they were just a handful of slugs, already surrounded and waiting to be mopped up. Out on the farming co-operatives American-built diesel tractors carried banners embroidered with the words, 'Yankees to the grave!'

Television aerials sprouted into the sky, as though a crop of roof-top onions had gone to seed, and beggars slept in doorways. The staircase of every hotel had a gate at the bottom which was kept locked; you could only come up or go down in the lift. In a hotel bathroom the C on a basin tap stood for cold, and the C on a shower tap for *caliente*; in the bidet both taps were marked C. Every Monday a culture supplement edited jointly by a novelist and a poet was included in the government newspaper, *Revolución*, which was otherwise mostly devoted to revolutionary invective, Castro's speeches and big pictures of the mangled victims of counter-revolutionary explosions—blown-up photographs of blown-up Cubans.

In an American-type cafeteria an unshaven *miliciano* with a pistol in his belt served hamburgers with home-fried potatoes and pumpkin pie. A troupe of minstrels came in, and apologetically offered a Cuban love-song, standing just inside the door. 'We will conquer the Yankee invader!' was written on a placard above their heads. One of them brought round a tin, showed the takings to the others; they shrugged, and filed out. But they were not sad.

C*

The dapper gentleman sitting in the same cafeteria and sipping a milk shake was reading the communist paper, *Hoy*; the old negro squatting outside against a pillar and chewing a piece of orange peel was reading the *Miami Herald*. A sallow man in a bus, with heavy eyelids and his hair caught in a bun and tied with a ribbon under a wide black sombrero, was reading *Man and Superman*. In the bookshops were the works of Orwell, Djilas, Colin Wilson, Lenin, Sartre, Pasternak and Erle Stanley Gardner.

Neon signs still advertised the capitalist firms—General Electric, the Royal Bank of Canada, Trans World Airlines—even though the firms had been banished. But they flickered half-heartedly, and every other bulb, or every other letter, was a blank. One of the few signs that burned steadily was over the entrance to the Russki Klub, but it was written in a language that no one could read. A beggar still stood outside the door of Woolworth's; the difference was that now the shop was nationalized—it belonged to him.

Hundreds of new Russian lorries stood in rows down at the docks; a huge Cadillac, only three or four years old, struggled asthmatically past them, making a noise like a big diesel tractor ploughing through heavy ground, and at about the same speed.

'No spare parts for two years,' moaned a man in a garage.

'No soap for two months,' moaned a woman at a party, adding that that sort of thing might be all right for the Russians, but in Cuba people liked to have a bath every day. She felt no affinity with Czechs or Ukrainians or North Koreans.

'No men for a week,' moaned a prostitute.

The news stands were covered with magazines from China, Poland, Rumania; in one bar *Time* magazine was on sale at three times the official price. In the British embassy was the *Illustrated London News*, and one of the staff said that what the Cubans liked best of all was the film of Princess Margaret's wedding. Once a month the British club met for lunch, and every month it was steak and kidney pie.

'Long live the First of May!' cried the headlines, with glorious optimism.

People danced in the carnival, but people also lived in fear; fear of denunciation, and of the G-2 agents who were only mentioned in whispers, who opened letters, tapped telephones, listened in the bars, knocked on the door in the early morning. The slaughter at the *paredón* went on—lives being blown out at dawn in the empty moat of La Cabaña fortress.

'Cuba will never forget this!' was written under an old photograph of two drunk American sailors climbing up the statue of José Martí. But in an airline office I had to pay an extra two dollars on my ticket, and the agent would accept nothing but American dollars. 'The customer is always right—so long as he doesn't attack the revolution' was painted over the counter, and outside the office a *miliciana* sat with a rifle on her lap, discourteously making every woman who entered open her handbag for a rough, unapologetic inspection.

A benign negro called Lázaro at the Ministry of Foreign Affairs said he was an ambassador-at-large by day (he was huge), and a medical student by night. He promised to organize a visit to a sugar factory for me. Nothing ever happened. A bank clerk called Victor, who wrote revolutionary poetry and psychological short stories, said he would ring up again later. He never did, and when I went to see him at his bank the sentry kept me waiting outside the door while he fetched Victor, who was embarrassed and explained that nationalization had brought so much extra work, and shook hands quickly and said he would ring up again later. He never did. A poet called Pablo promised to introduce me to Cuban poets, and a painter called René promised to introduce me to Cuban painters and a journalist called Juán and a film critic called Edmundo and a writer called Alejo said they would do everything they could to help me. But perhaps there was simply nothing they could do.

I had dozens of little conversations with people who asked all about me, and I told them, but when I asked all about them, they suddenly remembered about other things to do, and went away. One man who did help me was a sad-eyed American journalist called Bob who had been sacked by his paper for being too sympathetic towards the Cuban revolution and had stayed on in Havana, with a job in the government. He faced a prison sentence if he ever returned to the United States, and racked by both the conscience of a traitor and the agony of chronic dysentery his life was not happy. But his company was preferable to that of other foreign journalists and diplomats, hungering for political scandal and foretelling the crack of Cuban doom tomorrow; perhaps Bob was misguided, but at least he had more to offer Cuba than a sneer.

There were other people like Bob, from California and London and Sydney and Stockholm and Helsinki, all living in a hotel on the waterfront and working conscientiously for the Cuban revolution, but never quite qualifying for the same deference as the men from Moscow and Warsaw and Prague; and none of them were as venerated as the men from Peking.

Besides these earnest foreigners there were thousands of earnest Cubans too, but because they were working hard for their revolution and had no time to spare for inquisitive travellers they were difficult to meet. Much more approachable were the Cubans sitting in the bars, rows of them, throwing dice and shouting. They were indifferent, and they inspired indifference. They didn't like the regime, but they were not bothered enough to do anything about their dislike; they left it vaguely in the hands of the counter-revolution, or even of the United States. Some of them worked in nationalized businesses or government offices, and when I asked them how things were going and if their work had changed since the revolution, they would shrug, or even laugh. It was a joke, and these men had no responsibility, no conscience and no cares. I found it sad to hear of such chaos and inefficiency, and even more so when the situation was considered rather funny; but what was most sad of all was when the man who laughed also admitted that he went off to work every day in the uniform of a *miliciano*.

The paradoxes were endless. Some of them may not have been especially Cuban, but never having been in the New World before I didn't know how very new it was. Most of them, however, could never have been seen anywhere but in Cuba, in 1961. I like to think of the piles of scrubbed crabs and lobsters lying in the refrigerator of an expensive restaurant, and the boxes of strawberries at a dollar a helping, the melons, guavas, avocadoes, pomegranates, pineapples

76

and the tins of raspberries in syrup from Poland and salmon from Russia. Who was going to eat them all? I like to think of the waiters standing idle in a row against the polished mirrors, or dejectedly flicking a napkin over the tables, and the *daiquiri* machines growing rusty behind the bar. I like to think of a *daiquiri*, snow-cold in a glass.

I like to think of the dedicated co-operative manager telling me about his plans for the farm, and the sight of the new crops and the new buildings and the new, proud peasants. He wore a pistol in his belt, and I asked him if it was loaded. 'Of course,' he said, and pulled the trigger. I don't know where the bullet went.

I like to think of all the *bolas* and the threats and the boasts. Cuba was about to be invaded. Everybody said so. Just stay around for another week or two, they said, and you'll see. But I had stayed long enough and it was time to get on. I like to think of my last night in Havana, in the crowded cathedral square, under the Caribbean stars. In front of the old baroque façade the Russian cellist Rostropovich played Prokoviev. At the other end of the square dogs barked and children screamed, and old people living in cracked old buildings stood at their windows, bewildered by the orchestra under the floodlights, by the golden harp and the violins, and the extraordinary man from Russia playing a cello in their square.

III

Guatemala

THE FIRST PICTURE OF GUATEMALA IS A LAND-scape. In the bottom left-hand corner is a yellow petrol pump, and in the bottom right-hand corner is an Indian woman squatting in the shade of a bush. One cannot be certain what she is doing—defecating, or suckling a baby, or even having a baby; or just squatting in the shade of a bush. If you could see her face you would find that it was made of a kind of pale cellophane, discoloured by life and the sun almost to the brown of gold-beater's skin. Another woman walks past her, barefoot and bent under the weight of a baby in a bag on her back and a load of wood slung from a band round her forehead; she is dressed in a long blue skirt, striped and narrow, with a red embroidered shirt. A man walks with her, in a black jacket and black breeches to the knee, with crimson flaps on the outside edge and bare legs; he looks very aristocratic, like a rather ragged remnant of the Spanish conquistadors.

Behind is a little white-washed house with a shimmering jacaranda tree beside it and a blood-red bougainvillaea spilling across the roof. In the middle distance is a small coffee plantation, and beyond stretches the forest, ridge after ridge, with the twin white towers of a catholic convent marking the crest of the furthest ridge. The background is ruled by a volcano, its base lost in tropical mists and its cone perfectly dividing the sky. In one of the top corners soars an eagle, or perhaps it's a condor.

The next picture is a portrait of a very old man, but he is not a Guatemalan at all. He is a Dutchman, and he has spent fifty-five years as a shopkeeper in Central America. Now he is retired, and he sits alone in a wooden room lined with photos of heavy-faced men and women taken in Holland at the beginning of the century, prints of windmills and the waterfront at Delft, postcards from his granddaughter at school in Massachusetts, gramophone records and a small Dutch flag surrounded by plastic tulips. Through the open doorway, over a bank of brilliant bougainvillaea with humming-birds darting among the flowers, is Lake Atitlán, its surface changing as you look at it through every kind of shade from emerald to indigo; and on the far side, miles across the water, rise two symmetrical volcanoes, purple in the evening.

Suddenly a tourists' motor launch slips on to the lake, slitting open the surface like a surgeon's knife and folding it back in a brutal, widening gash. If the motor was not so noisy one might hear the click and whirr of a dozen cameras, desperately trapping the blues and greens before they fade.

When the boat has passed and Atitlán is left again to the humming-birds, the Dutchman points to the old photos on the walls and starts talking about his family, and particularly about his brother, who now runs a restaurant in Colorado but once accompanied Saint-Saëns to Egypt.

'I have a record of Samson and Delilah,' he says eagerly, and the opera rings through his little wooden room and out across the water.

'Perhaps I shall die here,' he says, when the record is finished and the volcanoes are vanishing into the night. 'Or perhaps I shall go somewhere else.'

Another picture is of Antigua, the old Spanish capital that was destroyed by an earthquake on July 29th, 1773. The churches and convents still stand, roofless and parched, noble under the sky. From the grass and weeds rise majestic pillars, spreading at the spandrels and lifting not a dome, but a huge disc of light, the sky itself. There is a special glory in an arch that no longer supports a roof or dangles a chandelier, but merely spans the sky. Traces of carving and fragments of green frescoes linger on the plaster, though they are nothing to the glimpse of a purple jacaranda over a ruined wall or a volcano through a window. The fountains in the cloisters are silent, and no nuns pass among the shadows; no candles, no incense, no bells, no echoes. The ruins are abandoned to

79

a few boys playing in the transepts, to the sun, and to the grandeur of their architecture.

Only in the crypt of the ruined cathedral, under the trim grass, does any ritual survive; the heat of so many candles, the thick stench of burning wax and the stark horror in the eyes of the mad old man tending them, drove me quickly back into the sunshine. In the roofless nave of a Jesuit church is a market, where women hook awnings to the pillars and spread out fruit, meat, clothes and Indian trinkets.

That is how I prefer my catholic churches, glorious and extinct—unlike my volcanoes. But there are signs that they may be only dormant; in the cathedral is a notice reading ' With God's help it will rise again ', and there are masons chipping at blocks of stone. Just as busy are the carpenters in an undertaker's across the road, hammering and planing in front of a stack of black polished coffins. Death is no stranger in Antigua.

The most familiar Guatemalan picture is of the market-place at Chichicastenango. It is market day, and the Indians have come down from their huts in the forest to sell and buy and worship. Men are weighing out beans, women are spinning wool, weaving rush mats and feeding their babies. A drunken Indian staggers shouting from a liquor stall, and starts fighting with another drunk; pathetically they tussle with each other, lunging for the other man's head and missing, each too drunk to score. A small crowd collects to watch them, but the spectators play no part, they don't even shout. Two *ladino* policemen appear and drag the drunks away, one of them already weeping from sickness and humiliation.

Through the square there is a steady, gentle chatter of voices. Poverty and peacefulness are the tones, only slightly jarred by the drunkards and the bright clothes. There are no rich merchants making profits from the Indians, and nobody shouts. Facing each other across the square are two white-washed churches, standing on stone plinths and reached by wide flights of steps. A man and his wife sit talking outside the smaller church, while she weaves a length of rope from dried reeds. What are they talking about? The god in the church? Their luck in the market? The funny woman

80

from Wisconsin who is taking photographs of them? They pack up their bags and walk in file out of the square, up to the hills, to worship a pagan god in the forest.

At the foot of the steps leading to the bigger church is a fire piled with logs, from which a blue pennant of smoke drifts across the white Spanish façade. Round the fire Indians stand muttering incantations with their eyes shut, or swinging incense in pots, or throwing powdered wood and aromatic sticks on to the embers; others are kneeling to pray. Beside the church is a convent cloister, with sad old trees struggling for life, and a door into the church.

Inside, all is candles. From the door to the altar is a bed of red and white rose petals, planted with thousands of candles, flickering on the floor and filling the church with a smoky yellow light and an acrid smell of wax, petals and piety. Round the candles are Indians, alone or in family groups, kneeling, praying, muttering, kissing; and in a dark corner of the church lurks a pale old man, dispensing advice, nostrums and blessing—a sort of terrible travesty of the confessor. Other figures peer from the gloom, with glints of baubles and tinsel, but they seem to be even less human than the old man, and they are probably made of wax. One of them is even crucified on a cross.

Tonight those Indians will all be back in the forest, worshipping other gods in other shrines, and lighting their candles for other idols. And tonight in the empty market-place at Chichicastenango a marimba band will strike up—a drum, a double bass and a gigantic xylophone attacked by five demoniac men—to shatter the village with tunes from a different, more violent world; but there will still be a scent of incense around the church steps, and two or three Indians to throw a last log on the fire and offer a last prayer, before wrapping up in their old wool rugs to sleep in the cold arcades.

Another picture is of Sixth Avenue in Guatemala City. There is a brass plate in the roadway, worn smooth by traffic but still proclaiming, 'Here died on June 26th, 1956, fighting for liberty and democracy . . .' and giving the names of four students. A tall young man wearing twill trousers and a blue blazer with a coat of arms on the pocket is looking down at it; he catches sight of me.

'Hello! You English too?' Neither of us could possibly be anything else.

After Cuba, I am surprised at the absence of negroes. Their place is taken by Indians, with guttural voices and obviously oriental faces, who give the street the flavour of some town in South-east Asia; the effect is increased by the shops and houses, low-built for fear of earthquakes, and the neon signs stretched between them almost excluding the sky and mocking the barefoot children, the begging women and the thin, ill-fed faces.

Indians, unlike negroes, don't walk very gracefully; they tend to amble along with their toes turned in. In Sixth Avenue one young woman, in gay Indian costume with a big bundle on her head, looks particularly ungainly, and as she crosses the road I see that she is wearing narrow shoes with high stiletto heels. She is in great pain. Transition, it seems, begins at the feet, with blisters, but she has a long long way to go. So has everything else in Guatemala; the yo-yo craze has only just hit the city, and smart young men are demonstrating them in shop doorways to crowds of gawping Indians.

At the end of the street is the main square. It is now Sunday morning and people are coming out of the cathedral doors into the sunshine. A dog slips out too, licking its lips. At the opposite end of the square a marimba band is playing in the concrete 'bowl', with a seven-man xylophone and a repertoire extending from Old Vienna to New Orleans; Marimba is the bane of Guatemala. A brass band is competing from under the trees, a group of evangelists is singing hymns, and the cathedral bells are ringing. An artist is holding an exhibition of his paintings—lurid crucifixes, doves, guitars, Indian girls. I have to pick the shoe-shine boys off my feet, like leeches. Guatemalans don't stare at me as much as Cubans did, but they have another habit which is much more unnerving; they take one look at me and then burst delightedly into laughter. Perhaps I should be happy to give so much pleasure. An old American resident is sitting on a bench talking to an old German resident.

'It was a beautiful funeral,' says the American. 'Very, very beautiful.'

The last picture of Guatemala is also the oldest. It is of Tikal, the ruined Maya city in the northern forests. The plane swoops over the trees and flops on to a grassy runway, and two American college girls in blue jeans step out of the jungle and stand blinking to greet us. The University of Pennsylvania has been working at Tikal for six years, scratching at the city.

The outlines of huge platforms a mile square can be traced in the jungle, with towers standing on them festooned with trees and foliage and reached by steep crumbling steps. It is the scale that most impresses; it is colossal. And it prompts the colossal question : what happened to the Mayas? They were not conquered, but it is known that they smashed much of their own city and then continued to live in it. Was it a revolution? The puzzle is more stunning than the monuments, for unfamiliarity makes the sculpture coarse, and ignorance of the Maya civilization doesn't heighten one's admiration of its jungle-swamped remains. In astronomy and mathematics they excelled, perhaps in other things too, but only three Maya manuscripts survived the fanaticism of the early Spanish priests, and the answer is buried as deep as the temples and altars of Tikal. However, as one of the American college girls says, 'It was definitely one of the greatest civilizations not only in the history of the entire world, but also in the history of the western hemisphere.'

*   *   *

A drunken Cuban went rolling down a street in Santiago de Cuba, lurching unsteadily and shouting, 'Para Fidel, paredón!' Nobody took any notice.

Three drunken soldiers staggered through the streets of Guatemala City singing, 'Viva Castro!' They were all arrested and sent to prison.

*   *   *

Officially, the British are unpopular in Guatemala. For Britain occupies the whole of Belice Province by force, and calls it British

83

Honduras. There are three empty seats in the Guatemalan assembly, draped with blue and white ribbons and marked 'Belice', and every map in Guatemala proves Britain's guilt. In the past Britain has offered to take the dispute to the International Court, but Guatemala has always refused; what the people who live in Belice feel is no concern of the Guatemalan government, and there is simply no arguing about the matter.

There are many matters in those parts about which there is simply no arguing, and one of them arose over a beauty competition for the title of Miss Central America. After a hasty priming of the judges the crown was awarded to Miss Belice, a nice plump coloured girl who was quite outclassed by the alluring Miss Panama, and the President of Guatemala made a special point of dancing with the winner; but she spoilt her coronation by signing her name boldly, Miss British Honduras.

I tried to meet the President, and called on his press secretary in the hideous green National Palace. He was a suave man with a diabolical wink. I mentioned something about land reform, and he immediately became defensive and got his secretary to make a copy of an article in an American newspaper praising Guatemala's efforts. Then he started to attack.

British Honduras was part of Guatemala, he said, and the Union Jack was only flying there temporarily. Very soon he would be able to invite me to the official hauling down and hoisting ceremony. How would it be achieved? Well, that was his secret, and he gave me one of his winks. I asked him if I could have an appointment with the President, and he said no, because the President didn't want to meet any more Englishmen. The last one, after an interview, had written some articles in his paper about a funny little man running a funny little country, and if that was the British idea of funny ... The secretary winked again.

I suggested that perhaps I could approach the President direct, and he said that, indeed, I was perfectly free to send him a telegram asking for an interview, but somehow he didn't think that it would be much use. And he winked.

'The President would ask me who you are, and I would tell him.

You see, I am the Goebbels of Guatemala.' And then he added, as if to make it sound more endearing, ' You remember, Goebbels was the cleverest of the Nazis.' And he winked again.

I reminded him of Goebbels' fate, and of course I never met the President. A few days later in the official government newspaper, edited by that same press secretary, there was a paragraph under the heading ' English Education' describing how we, in the newspaper office, were informed one morning that there was an Englishman in the anteroom asking to see us, and we called him in. He entered, a fair-haired man about two metres high with a magnificent Oxford accent—but no jacket; while he was asking questions we pondered on the reaction of the door-keeper at the Ministry of Information in London if a ' savage' from Guatemala had permitted himself the liberty to address him, though only a door-keeper, in his shirt-sleeves.

*   *   *

Julio, who was once a newspaperman but now worked for the American embassy, told me about the President's press secretary. ' I don't like him. Nobody likes him. He has no friends.' Julio didn't like the government either, and told me so.

I went with him to the ceremonial presentation of fifty new houses to their tenants—part of a big housing scheme on the outskirts of Guatemala City. A third of the cost had been paid by the American government, a third by the Guatemalan government, and a third was to be paid by the tenants themselves in the form of a monthly rent for twenty years, after which the houses would become their own property. It was a truly co-operative scheme, with the tenants building the houses in their spare time under supervision from American foremen.

The American ambassador arrived in a jeep, and the President drove up an hour later in his armour-plated Cadillac with inch-thick bullet-proof windows, and the band played the national anthem and then the Star Spangled Banner. Flustered officials looked round sternly for the Archbishop of Guatemala, and decided to go on

85

without him. The President made a speech; so did the ambassador; rockets and squibs exploded, the band played on, the flags tugged at their masts and the fifty lucky men stepped to the platform, shook hands with the President and took from him their title deeds, shook hands with the ambassador and took from him their latch-key. It was all most moving.

Julio too was moved. On the way home he asked me to forget everything he had said about the Guatemalan government, because he was now working for the American government and was not allowed to have any opinions. And the press secretary? Yes, he was a good man, a very good man. Everybody liked him.

'He is my friend.'

*   *   *

The most important men in Guatemala, said a newspaper editor, were the President and the Archbishop. They represented the two forces, the army and the church, which militated most strongly against the likelihood of any Castro-type revolution in Guatemala. The officers of both were determined to maintain their ranks and privileges, and the rich Guatemalans were doing all they could to help. The third most important man, he added, was the American ambassador.

That editor and a lawyer were the two most vehement, but reasonable, critics of the government I met. They were disillusioned with America, with American interference in Guatemalan politics, with the American-owned businesses and public utility companies, with the privileges and concessions which American businessmen demanded, and with the conditions which America put on Guatemala's trade and economy. There were signs, they admitted, of a change of heart, and though the businessmen were still a long way behind at least the officials who came from America nowadays were a little more realistic and understanding. Some of them had even learnt to speak Spanish.

Cuba, of course, was always the main topic. Liberal Guatemalans, they said, looked at Cuba with sympathy, not with hatred or distrust, but a little saddened that such an affliction should have struck a Latin American sister—and particularly one whom they had always loved and admired so much. But there was real resentment that the United States had tried to meddle in Cuba—let Cuba look after herself, even if she is communist—and even more resentment that Guatemala should have been used as a training-ground for an attack against Cuba.

Guatemala's destiny, said the lawyer, was not with the United States, but with Latin America. Nationalism was the first motive, but it was supported by a strong affinity with Chile, Uruguay, Brazil and Mexico, where things were happening that had a far deeper appeal to Guatemalan emotions than anything America could provide. The republics of Central America had recently formed a vague economic alliance which one day might grow into a political federation—and that was an encouraging sign.

'It's partly a question of psychology, and partly a question of rhythm. They play the same sort of music down there.' And then, to explain his own position, he said, 'I'm on the left; but of course not nearly so far left as your Labour Party.'

Guatemalans, said the editor, were divided between the anti-Castro, the pro-Castro and the indifferent. The anti-Castro were the tiny minority of rich people, who were understandably aware of Castro's appeal to the poor and of his danger to themselves. But instead of making any attempt to answer that appeal with an alternative one, they did exactly what the rich people of Cuba had done; they put their faith in the army and the church, and their money into foreign investments. They hadn't learnt any lessons from Cuba—except that 'it can't happen here'—and they only thought of Cubans as having to suffer a peculiarly Cuban misfortune. They had no social conscience, and they had no common sense.

The pro-Castro Guatemalans were an even tinier minority of students, intellectuals and out-of-work white-collar workers. Only a few of them were actually in touch with Havana and Moscow, but the rest saw in Castro a chance of breaking the age-old, stifling rule by millionaires and military presidents. They admired him for smashing the army, which in so many Latin American countries takes up too much money and too many useful people, and they admired him still more for laughing, in front of the whole world, at the United States.

As for the indifferent, they were just the entire people of Guatemala—the huge majority of peasants, workers and Indians who were mostly illiterate and whose lives had scarcely changed in four hundred years. Politics meant nothing to them, and they were as ignorant of the difference between a dictatorship and a democracy as they were of the name of their own President. But recently, in the last few years, they had heard about a man in Cuba, wherever that was, who had taken land from the rich and given it to the poor, and who had cut down rents, and who must be a good man.

The lawyer maintained that it wasn't a simple choice between East and West. Guatemalans—and all Latin America for that matter—should take what it wanted from both, from the United States, from Britain, from India, from Japan, from China, and then add something of its own. Perhaps, he said hopefully, the Cuban revolution would turn out to be the key which, though not the answer itself, would open a future of better, bigger ideas. Perhaps Castro was the catalyst that was needed to make possible the best of all revolutions—radical, beneficent and, alas, so far unknown. There was a chance, he felt, and even a few small signs for hope; but there were other signs, too, which suggested that the very people who should have been provoked by Castro into becoming champions of a new enlightenment, had in fact been petrified into inaction.

'Where are the Mayas now?' the lawyer cried. 'Look what they did a thousand years ago, in the forest at Tikal! That's what we need—a faith, a purpose and a little energy.'

'The best things in the Cuban revolution,' added the editor, less eloquently, 'could all have been achieved by democracy.'

But the fact is, of course, they never were.

*   *   *

Several hundred demonstrators, mostly young, marched into the cathedral square one evening. Some of them shouted, '*Cuba Sí*,

Yankees No!' and two of them carried a big poster with a picture of Castro pushing Uncle Sam along in a wheelbarrow, the old man's testicles hanging over the edge of the barrow.

They stopped in a corner of the square near a poster advertising a bull-fight, and after two or three speeches, cheered by the crowd that had collected to watch, a man announced that they were now going to burn an effigy of President Kennedy. A sheet of paper was held up, on which a portrait of Kennedy, grinning bravely, had been painted, and the crowd shouted, 'Cuba Sí!' A girl in trousers struck a match with a shrill war-cry, but it was straightaway blown out. She struck another and quickly put it to the corner of the paper. There was a breathless moment, and then a terrific flame shot up, with a cloud of black smoke. The crowd yelled, 'Cuba Sí!'

But the paper wouldn't burn properly, and when the flames died out, there was Kennedy, still grinning. More matches were struck, while the crowd went on chanting 'Cuba Sí!' like a pianist holding a long chord and waiting for the singer to begin. There was another flash, and at last the paper began to burn. It was flung flaming into the air, tossed over the crowd's heads, and torn to bits; and the charred pieces were carried triumphantly through the streets of Guatemala City.

Half an hour after the demonstration broke up, the plate glass windows of the United Fruit Company of Boston were smashed. And next evening the same people turned up to demonstrate again.

Next evening, however, they were met by another party, unofficial but armed with guns, and within a few minutes fifteen of the demonstrators had been wounded and three were dead.

'But at least the demonstration was not forbidden,' said a Guatemalan.

'But the United Fruit Company is no longer the bugaboo it used to be,' said an American.

'But you know, death means nothing in these countries, really,' said an Englishman.

El Salvador

EL SALVADOR IS KNOWN AFFECTIONATELY AS THE
Ruhr of Central America, but I can't believe the Ruhr is anything
like so exciting. In El Salvador eighty-two per cent of the population
is born illegitimate, seventeen per cent of the women who enter
hospital are found to have syphilis, and the second most popular
cause of death, after gastritis, is homicide. Over the whole country,
lost in ethereal mists of wealth, privilege and nepotism, swim the
Fourteen Families.

' It's more like Forty,' said one man.

' There are really only Four,' said another. But however many
the families number, theirs is the republic, the power and the glory,
and for ever and ever they mean to keep it. Beneath this thin upper
crust, perilous like an over-risen soufflé, lies a steamy hollow in
which lives the tiny middle class, and far below, at the bottom of
the pot, in poverty and social anarchy, is the pudding. Between the
few thousands of people who own a car, and the two million who
don't even have a pair of shoes, there is almost nobody.

But the fact that there is a middle class at all makes El Salvador a
little different from the rest of Central America. There is a handful
of Germans, French, Italians and Arabs, as well as Salvadoreños,
who have built up export, import or retail businesses or small industries, and though most of them may not be very rich they constitute a core of prosperity which gives El Salvador the title of Ruhr
and makes it respected and slightly feared by the other republics,
who feel that in any future Central American federation the smallest
member would steal the show.

The British ambassador threw up his hands. In six months he had
dealt with four different administrations. The latest was a trium-

virate of two colonels and one civilian. 'Who is telling them what to do? Who is pulling the strings? You and I know what soldiers are like; they couldn't possibly do it on their own. If you can find out who is controlling them you have the answer to El Salvador.'

The triumvirate had suspended the constitution, and in desperation had forbidden the millionaires to send any more money out of the country. 'It's so stupid,' said one of the millionaires. 'It will only make the peasants think we're frightened of them, and then they will start getting out of control, and then nobody will invest their money in El Salvador.' Money, money, money.

'It used to be such a peaceful, happy little country,' said an elderly Dutch woman, wiping her hands on her skirt after driving a beggar boy away from her doorway. 'Anybody could make money here—anybody. I fled from the Nazis twenty years ago and came here without a cent. Now look; I have all this property, and I fly to Europe every summer. The beggars? They needn't be poor if they don't want to be. They only have to work. I *worked*. They can go to an institution and get food. There are special places for them; they don't have to beg. I subscribe to a charity, so I never give anything to beggars. And they can go to a school to learn to read if they want to, or learn a trade. They are just too lazy to earn any money.' Money, money, money.

Castro had gone and spoilt it all. 'Castro is the biggest thing in these parts since Independence in 1821,' said an American information officer, after lamenting that though the triumvirate could stop the flight of capital they couldn't stop the flight of intelligence. Local education was a joke, and the university, where the professors were just a jump ahead of the students, produced only a tiny dribble of graduates; too many Salvadoreños who had been educated abroad never came back. But quite apart from the attractions of communism and the natural popularity of a man who had tweaked the gringos' tail, Castro had become the focus of every discontent and the outlet of every pent-up frustration. Even the peasants had heard of a man who was giving things away to other peasants—land, houses, a better chance, an alternative; he was a light in the dark when they had never dared hope—when it had never occurred to them to hope—that the night would ever end. And whether it was myth or reality, it was kept alive by clever communist tactics.

Two Salvadoreños I met had two very different opinions. The first was an elderly newspaper editor called Napoleon, who said that it was more important for a country to be strong than to be democratic, because only strength would destroy communism and even an atomic war was better than communism. These new restrictions on capital were dangerous as well as useless, because they betrayed El Salvador's instability to the world and would discourage foreign investors. Industrialization and increased production were the answers, not hasty controls and taxation. Reform could only come with a change of heart, a higher moral conscience and a more realistic approach to economic development. It was the same with wages; if wages on the coffee plantations were raised it would only create unemployment, for the plantation owners who employed more labourers than they really needed would have to dismiss many of them. Napoleon himself had had similar trouble with his maids at home; an attempt had been made to enforce minimum wage rates for domestic servants and he had had to cut down his staff, who were admittedly underpaid but who were also underworked. He had more fine, Napoleonic things to say; and really El Salvador had been getting along quite nicely until that traitor in Cuba started upsetting it all.

The other Salvadoreño was a socialist who had once been invited to Moscow at Russia's expense, but on the way he had had second thoughts; he had stopped off in England and travelled through western Europe instead. Soon after his return to El Salvador he had been exiled to Honduras, but after a change in the government he had been allowed back again. He was an Anglophile, democratic, idealistic and patriotic; and he was in a hurry. El Salvador had a long way to catch up, and it had to be done quickly. Education was the thing; the people must be taught not only to read and write but also to understand.

Cuba, he felt, was a tragedy. Many of the reforms were fine and necessary, but Castro had betrayed the revolution and sold his country to the communists. Poor Cubans! However, Castro was

92

a Cuban too, and the United States had no right to interfere. El Salvador's problems were not quite the same as Cuba's had been; the Indians were far more primitive than any Cuban peasant, and in El Salvador there was a population problem, with a shortage of land, that Cuba had never experienced. But the important thing was that each country should be left to work out its problem for itself. Latin Americans were intensely sensitive, and North Americans were palpably unaware of it. And if the United States should make so much fuss about the tyranny of a left-wing dictator like Castro, why didn't they do anything about right-wing dictators like Trujillo of the Dominican Republic and Somoza of Nicaragua, who were just as villainous in the eyes of liberal Latin Americans?

Other Latin American countries, he argued, might be justified in interfering, particularly if they could unite and wage a joint campaign. But bitterly he confessed that there was little chance of any such unity; too many governments were ruling against the will of the people. Men of vision and imagination always found themselves up against a great wall of ignorance and selfishness, and they were either persecuted out of existence, or else they gave up the fight and succumbed to the same weaknesses as their predecessors—for the best men in the world were only human, and Latin Americans were the most human of them all.

The tragedy of El Salvador was a magnification of this man's own personal tragedy. They all knew, he said, what was needed: the country should be united, modernized, stabilized, industrialized, purged of corruption, and the cycle of military dictators should be finally broken. They were all aware of the facts, of the needs and of the dangers of delay. The poignancy of their tragedy lay in their incurable pride; they were too touchy to let anybody else pull them out of the mess, but they knew that they were quite incapable of doing it themselves. Between the need and the execution was a terrible, uncrossable gap of personal ineffectiveness and futility.

*   *   *

Poor old Cotton Joe. He had died a week ago. Nobody quite knew what his job had been—something to do with cotton, they said—but for years he had stood at the window of the Casa Clark and watched the girls go by. Some evenings he went off to a brothel and didn't come back till breakfast time. But his real vice was vodka—five bottles a week, and it killed him.

I have a fellow feeling with old Cotton Joe. The Casa Clark would drive me to vodka, and perhaps to the brothel too. The proprietor eagerly showed me round, watching my face for signs of friendship. He showed me the refrigerator and told me to help myself to a beer from it when I wanted one and just sign a chit, because everything was free-and-easy here. He explained about the communal towels in the bathroom, because we only allowed decent people to stay here, and about the arrangements in the dining-room where the guests were arranged at tables with other guests to create a proper family spirit and where everybody helped themselves to food from the sideboard, and to as many helpings as they liked; for nobody went hungry at the Casa Clark. And of course there was no need to lock the door of my room at night; in fact there was no key in the door, because all of us were friends here. On the walls were little pictures of purple volcanoes framed in bamboo, and rustic notices like ' God bless our mortgaged house.'

At supper I was introduced to lots of cheery Americans and even cheerier Germans, and we ate good American steaks, drank iced tea and ended up with blackberry-and-apple squashed under a square of fibre-board. None of that dreadful local food. I only wished old Cotton Joe had managed to hang on for another ten days, and next morning I moved to a rattling old hotel in the middle of the town, where traffic roared past my window all day and neon signs flashed into it all night. Dust lay deep everywhere, and there were fleas in the bed; women too, I was told, for a small supplementary charge.

One night I was woken by the whole room rattling round me. The walls and the windows were quivering, and the furniture was jumping like dice in a box. I knew at once that it wasn't a dream, though I had never been in an earthquake before. It lasted for about ten seconds, and during that time I was angry and terrified and fascinated; angry at being woken up, terrified that it might be really dangerous, and fascinated by a curious passive pleasure and by my own impotence. I was the object of a huge inhuman force, and I found it thrilling. When it stopped I wanted it to go on. But nothing happened at all, except that a man in the empty square outside shouted for joy.

One morning I looked out and saw a most alluring girl in a tight dress clipping on her high heels across the square towards the market; her brown hair floated on her shoulders, in one hand she carried a smart plastic handbag, and the other was steadying a huge bundle of vegetables on her head. And one evening I spent drinking *tic-tac*, a raw cane spirit made palatable by lime juice, in the company of a crowd of disillusioned young Salvadoreños. In turn they got up and sang maudlin songs or recited their own poems. Only one of them had a girl with him; the others poured all their love into songs and poetry. The girl said, 'The United States is the best country in Latin America.'

Another earthquake happened when I was sitting with a diplomat in the American embassy, but he didn't interrupt his sentence. He just went on talking. And in the Post Office one afternoon an unbelievable Englishman, with no chin and a bull terrier on a lead, came up to me: 'I say, excuse me, sir; but I suppose your name isn't Montgomery by any chance?'

*   *   *

'I went to school at Harrow-on-the-Hill. But not the school that you mean; there's another one that nobody's ever heard of. I was working as an office boy in London in 1926. The General Strike drove me out. All those bloody people doing nothing. So I came to El Salvador. My brother was working for the railway here; it's British, you know. Now I've got my own business: agencies, accounting and a bit of journalism. Democracy? What, *here*? It's a lot of bloody eyewash. They aren't fit to vote. Give a Salvadoreño a little money and he spends it on *tic-tac*. Then he goes and screws a woman. The women can't resist it. None of 'em. Before the Spaniards came to Central America there was an invasion by an Indian tribe from the north, who found another tribe already settled here; they intermarried, but somehow they stayed separate too, so that often you got the men in a family speaking one language and the women another. Then the Spaniards came in on top. Result—bloody anarchy. Christ, man! Look at those tits! Have you ever seen such a pair? Bloody marvellous. But you take off that bra and what've you got, eh? what've you got? The Indians used to appease the gods of the harvest every year by drowning four virgins in Lake Ilopango. But they don't do it now. They ran out of virgins. I don't believe there's a virgin in the whole bloody country. Oh, yes, we've got tabloid papers and strip cartoons and banks and big coffee profits and French-fried bloody popcorn machines and cosy suburbs and swimming-pools with lots of lovely brown girls arsing around and all that stuff. But beyond that, what've you got, eh? It's just the same as when the Spaniards came. Worse, really. You take this ban on exporting capital. It's just spite, aimed at a few rich people who did it once or twice too often and sent too much money to the States. Currency control, my fanny! Do you know what I'd do? I'd put 'em in the *tubo*. You don't know what the *tubo* is? It's a tube, see. It's a long, narrow, high passage in the middle of the police station, with a door at each end. Put a bloke in it one evening without his trousers on, and put forty or fifty perverts in it with him—you know, the kind you get in any prison. By breakfast time he's been buggered about thirty-six times. It works. They do it often. It's the same with all these people they banish. Whenever there's a change of government a lot of people have to go into exile. Communists go to Cuba, but they're not wanted there either, because they've been a failure here, and they get thrown out of Cuba too. Other people go to Costa Rica or Mexico, and some of them are even given jobs in embassies for a few years, and then allowed back again. But what's the bloody sense in exiling people? It's always the clever ones who have to go, and we need the clever ones here. I'd put 'em in the *tubo*. Just for a night. That'd sort 'em out. The people? All they want is another drink. And a bit of tail. A vote? Christ, man. A boy and a girl live together for a few years, and have a couple of children. He

Waiting for Castro

CUBA

Lottery ticket seller

CUBA

Militia

CUBA

Terrorists and traitors to the wall!

CUBA

GUATEMALA

Indian market at Chichicastenango

GUATEMALA   Futility

The Ruhr of Central America

El Salvador

Traffic

HONDURAS

Shoe-shine

HONDURAS

Bay Island village

HONDURAS   The mask of the Mayas

Post Office

Costa Rica

The Switzerland of Central America

Desolation

PANAMA

Rum and washing

The capital

HAITI

Soap-seller

The Citadel

Haiti

The market

DOMINICAN REPUBLIC   The streets are clean

DOMINICAN REPUBLIC   After Mass

La Perla

Puerto Rico

Toyshop

leaves her, she goes on the streets, the kids become beggars, and he becomes a thief. It's all rotten, down to the bottom. The rich? All they want is more money, and a third car. Corruption? Christ, yes! Any amount. A month ago the whole central market went up in flames. All the stalls, all the stock, everything—the lot. Destroyed. An accident? Perhaps. The government said the communists did it. The communists said the government did it, and I shouldn't be surprised; to clean it up, move it somewhere else, because they reckoned there was too much conspiracy going on in it. But who suffers? Not the communists. Not the government. The poor bloody people. I tell you, the only really patriotic people in El Salvador are the army officers. They come from all classes, and the best ones come from poor families, which means that they're not at all in love with the rich families. Until they get rich themselves, of course. They're not particularly clever—what soldier is? But they have a tradition of always appointing the rulers, and they're passionately jealous of it. Christ, yes, they're passionate. If anyone tries to interfere with them, they bite. They turned out the last President because he was breaking the rules and beginning to annoy the more progressive men in the army. Then they put in the Junta—six left-wing officers; but they saw straight away that they were giving in to the Fidelistas and the communists, so they got rid of the Junta and set up the Directorio—three officers and two civilians. A few weeks later they sacked two of them, and now we've got this lot—two colonels and a lawyer. But you can bet your life it's not those three who are making the decision. It's the young officers—the captains. The army's the only bloody thing that's constant in politics here. They're patriotic and sincere, and almost incorruptible. In a way they're a good thing; they don't support the millionaire families, and their pride gives them the nearest thing to a conscience you'll find in El Salvador. But, of course, they're conservative, and they won't let anyone take away their power. They saw what Castro did to the Cuban army; he cut down the regular army and gave guns to all the people instead. Guns aren't legal in this country, but everyone carries one who can afford it. I never invite Salvadoreños to take their coats off when they come to my house, because they mostly wear shoulder holsters and they would be embarrassed. Poor people carry knives, but it's so messy; you have to wipe the blade afterwards, and then you have to get your handkerchief washed. It's pretty uncivilized. Have you been to the British Club? They play the best game of snooker in Latin America there. The new port at Acajutla? I give it three months. It'll be washed about thirty-six miles up the bloody Pacific coast. He ought to be put in the *tubo*, the man who designed it.'

We were standing on a hill at night, looking over San Salvador, the capital. The city lights crept out in a check pattern of streets and avenues to the foot of the hills, and volcanoes stood against the stars. Suddenly, a mile below us, a rocket rose from the darkness and exploded into coloured lights, the bang just reaching our ears. More fireworks followed, and people shouted.

' I hope to Christ they're enjoying themselves down there. There's not much bloody fun in El Salvador, if you're poor.'

*   *   *

Aching for four hours on a crowded wooden bench in a railway carriage rattling to Acajutla I thought of the owners, sitting in their smoke-bound offices in the City of London. How many of them had ever taken a ticket and meandered down their line, among the volcanoes and through the coffee plantations, the coffee bushes shiny under special shade trees like lettuces under cloches? Market women with radishes, onions, chickens, babies and dogs filled the carriage with laughter and a smell of sweat. An old lunatic yattered away sadly to herself; children sucked their fingers and stared at me.

We passed Izalco, the volcano that had erupted every ten minutes for centuries. The Lighthouse of the Pacific, it was called, for its regular explosion of flame and cascade of molten lava could be seen by ships far out to sea, and it had become El Salvador's only tourist attraction. The government, advertising ' the Volcano of Izalco who erupts regularly his spectacular burst of fire, smoke and lava, followed by distant rumblings ', built a new road up a

98

neighbouring mountain and a big modern hotel on top, so that tourists could gloat over the old man's performance in comfort. But just as the hotel was finished and before it was even opened, impotence struck and Izalco stopped. The hotel stands there, empty and unused, and people wonder uneasily where the gases that used to burst every ten minutes are now accumulating.

The whole of El Salvador seemed to be spending its Sunday at the new port of Acajutla, which had been opened with a great flourish two days before. The ocean wind picked up cement dust and cardboard packages and girls' skirts, and the harsh white sun glared on the concrete warehouses, on the Pacific breakers, and on the stark paint and naked guns of an American destroyer, lying against the new wharf like a first lover.

I met an old man in the wide straw hat of a picture-book Mexican, with a little boy, his grandson. They had come all the way from Santa Ana to see the new port. Together we walked two miles through the sun and wind and dust to the old village of Acajutla, where Pedro de Alvaredo was nailed to his wooden saddle by an Indian arrow in 1523. Cars rolled past us through the dust, faces pressed to the dusty windows and radios muffled by the dust. The old man talked about coffee. Now that there was a port the ships would no longer have to anchor out beyond the surf and wait for lighters to bring the coffee out to them; the old black barges lying fat and blistered in their sheds above the beach would never be launched again.

'Why don't you in England buy our coffee? It's the best in the world, you know. But you get all yours from Africa. In Africa they grow it without shade trees, but we can't do that in El Salvador. We've tried.' Then he added, wistfully, 'How much does it cost to fly to England?'

I sat in a café overlooking the black sand beach. Screaming bathers, coloured umbrellas, leggy girls in bikinis, American cars with transistor radios—and ragged barefoot children waiting near my table for the scraps of rice and shrimp shells from my plate. I drank too many beers, to wash down the dust and to wash away the muddle of thoughts provoked by the bikinis, the beggars and

99

the City men in blue suits and City typists in knitted cardigans sitting in an office far away.

*　　　*　　　*

In 1888 a man from Bethlehem, a Christian Arab who was travelling through Central America selling mother o' pearl cruci-fixes and souvenirs from the Holy Land, found himself stranded in El Salvador with a bad debt. The debt was eventually paid in cotton cloth, and the Arab rented a doorway in the market-place, spread out his bales and sold them for a big profit. Immediately he decided to give up being a travelling salesman; he sent for his family, and as the business grew other relations and their friends came out to join him. Now there are twelve thousand Arabs from Bethlehem in El Salvador.

One of them is called Solomon, a splendidly salacious young man with fat black eyebrows, a passion for making money and another passion for spending it on women. On my last night in the country he offered to take me round the brothels of San Salvador. We went to four.

The first was the cheapest and also the happiest. Solomon rang the bell—two longs and a short—of a dingy unlit house in a suburb; a little grille in the green iron door, over which was written ' Pension ', was opened and two eyes looked out into ours. Solomon was recognized, and we were let in. Inside was a room opening on to a courtyard with potted plants and benches. There were girls everywhere—simple, friendly, unsophisticated, beautiful girls, sitting around waiting. They might have been waiting for a dance, or to see the doctor. Two or three men were sitting on the benches, drinking beer with one arm round a snuggling girl. On the walls were coloured prints of Christ and the Virgin Mary. Occasionally the street bell rang—two longs and a short—and a girl opened the grille to look out, before letting in another customer, or one of her colleagues. The girls were as efficient and professional as waitresses or typists, and infinitely funnier. We drank a lot of beer with them.

The second was a much more plush place, with a man in charge of the bar, and a prominent staircase going up to the first floor. The girls had smarter clothes and dyed hair; they hummed American tunes and chewed gum. They had lost more than their innocence.

After more beer we went on to the third brothel, which was grander still—a private house with a little patio and only three girls, dressed like debutantes and lounging in contemporary aluminium chairs with magazines. They didn't look up when we came in. There was no beer, only Scotch, and Solomon said that there were no bedrooms either; the girls expected to be taken home, or to a hotel. He had once taken one of them out for the night, and next day he had met her again in a commercial office, where she was a secretary; she had laughed at his surprise, and explained that she went to the brothel two or three times a week, just as other girls might go to the pictures, or for a swim.

The last brothel made a brave attempt to look like a guest-house. There were bedrooms all round a wide quadrangle, and an old woman yawning with boredom and impatience, hobbling round putting bottles of beer in a huge, ticking refrigerator. Solomon's favourite girl was out, and he gnashed his fat eyebrows with fury; she was having dinner with a friend, said the old hag, but you never knew, she might be back later. We sat down and ordered beer.

The only other man in the place was a pilot in the air force. He was very drunk, far beyond enjoying the girls; all he wanted was more beer. He talked about his flying, over the volcanoes and out across the Pacific. Then he mentioned an uncle—'They say he's going to be the next President'—but it wasn't just beer that made him sound so indifferent. Politics were left to the politicians, and even a man flying for his country, and one day perhaps fighting for it, knew that the matter would be settled without anybody ever asking for his opinion. He submitted totally, and he didn't even complain.

Outside the lavatory I found a book on a window sill. It was published in Argentina and was called *Poesía Sexual*; I took it away, to save me from having to listen to the pilot, but there was a swift rustling of bedding and a vague figure appeared through the black window-frame. A man's voice said, in impeccable English, 'Would you mind giving me my book back, please?' I went back to Solomon and the pilot, and we drank more beer. The old woman at last couldn't stand it any more. 'If only you would all go to bed, or go away.' In the end we went away.

V

Honduras

'WHAT ARE YOU TRAVELLING IN?' ASKED AN Englishman at Tegucigalpa airport. I found it difficult to tell him. He was travelling in Scotch, himself, and doing quite well.

'In these countries you can always tell how important a town is by its statues,' he said. 'In the smaller towns they only have a bust of their hero, with a few flower beds round him. The more important places make a proper full-length job of him. And if he's on a horse . . .'

In Tegucigalpa he's on a horse, in the cathedral square, swiping the air with his sword. The bronze figure was ordered from Italy, and when it arrived they discovered that it was the wrong man; but he was very splendid and nobody minded, so they kept him. Around him, on stone benches in the shade of the trees, sit all the men of Honduras, talking under their wide straw hats and having their shoes cleaned. If you sit on one of the benches the shoe-shine boys settle on you like flies, and if you move along they buzz along with you; you have to swat them, or flick them off with the back of your hand.

Further on, students play football in front of the old university, and beyond the new Congress building, the best piece of modern architecture I saw in Central America, the hill falls steeply to the river. You can look down narrow streets to the river—but it's not much more than a smelly river-bed with women washing their clothes in the filthy trickle below the bridges—and beyond to the mountains. Tegucigalpa is surrounded by mountains.

Above the river stands the President's palace, a fantastic child's fort, with turrets and battlements and sentries dozing over their bayonets, and apologies to Balmoral, New Delhi, Saint Pancras and the Alhambra. It was hard to believe that any serious President could have the face to live in such a sugar-plum castle.

But the President of Honduras, I was assured, was a very serious man indeed. On his silver wedding day the whole diplomatic corps was summoned to high mass in the cathedral, in the middle of which the Papal Nuncio presented him and his wife with a signed photograph of the Pope.

Tegucigalpa has style. It is like a rather seedy Italian town without the tourists. After Guatemala City and San Salvador, which had both been destroyed by earthquakes and timidly rebuilt with bungalows, I longed for heights and elevations, and in Tegucigalpa I found elegant squares, white-fronted churches, and tall houses with pretty girls sitting sewing in doorways or hanging out of upper windows. At last there were upper windows to hang out of.

There were schoolgirls in white blouses and grey pleated skirts, and nuns in white robes, and traffic policemen standing on little red platforms with little red umbrellas over them, painted with Coca-Cola advertisements, and a woman walking down a steep street carrying a huge water-melon on her head. Of three couples whose names were pinned to the cathedral door announcing their banns of marriage, two bridegrooms and one of the brides were illegitimate. Popsicles were for sale, and I would have bought a dozen if I had known what they were. Tiny little buses raced down the streets with a boy in the back shouting out of the window for passengers. And nobody knew the way to anywhere.

In the O. Henry bar, the beer was pale and weak, like old potato water, but so cold that it didn't matter. Americans were drinking it out of the bottle—the barman didn't even bother to give them a glass. One of the Americans was wearing my old school tie.

In Tegucigalpa it was difficult to be bothered with the business of finding-out-the-facts. It was the kind of place which makes one feel on holiday. But I did go to see a newspaper editor, and I asked him the usual questions about Cuba and the effect of its revolution on Honduras. The trouble with Castro, he said, was that he had been such a distraction, and politicians in other countries had wasted too much time wondering whether they were for him or against

104

him, instead of getting on with their own problems; while others had said, 'Thank God for Castro; he's woken us up at last.'

But Honduras' problems are very different from El Salvador's. El Salvador is a small, crowded country with a coast only on the Pacific. Honduras is a big empty country which faces naturally towards the Caribbean, and which has no land problem and no millionaires; the money has been made by the big American fruit companies, not by Hondureños. It is the archetypal banana republic, and its chief need, after education and health and better communications, is to find something else to do besides grow bananas.

*   *   *

The Caribbean coast of Honduras, compared with the volcanic uplands of the rest of the country, belongs to a different world: a world of dazzling, untrodden beaches, of tiny steamy ports, of laughing negroes; a world of inland swamps and lagoons, with canoes floating on them like water-beetles, their paddles resting leg-like on the viscous surface; a world redolent of pirates and the stories of O. Henry; a world, above all, of the banana. Huge plantations languish over the coastal plan, cut by narrow-gauge railways leading to the ports, and even if ivory-faced men in the air-conditioned offices of The Company tell you that the Honduras banana business is going down the drain, there are still an awful lot of bananas to go.

But it was not bananas that I was after as I stood one Saturday morning on the scorching iron pier at La Ceiba. Monday was to be a holiday and I asked the British ambassador in Tegucigalpa what would be a good way of spending a long weekend. 'Go to the Bay Islands,' he said without hesitation. They had belonged to Britain, he said, until 1859, when a generous Queen had discarded an unusually valueless possession as a mark of her philanthropy. One of his predecessors at the embassy, some years ago, had been there, and in his report, among other compliments, he had written that the women of the islands were reputed to be the most passionate in the world. The present incumbent, too, had paid a visit with his

D*   105 wife to the easternmost island, Guanaja, and recommended the trip. A plane, he said, left Tegucigalpa for Guanaja every Saturday, and returned on Monday.

But when I went to the airline office I was told that the service had been stopped months ago, because nobody used it, and the best I could do would be to fly to La Ceiba and hope for a boat across to Guanaja. 'Oh yes,' said the ravishing *ladino* girl, fluttering an absurdly extravagant pair of eyelids, 'plenty of boats.' And she sold me a ticket to La Ceiba.

In the aeroplane half the passengers were Congressmen going to attend the opening of a new milk plant, and the other half were priests going to an apostolic convention. One of the politicians said that Fidelism was the same as communism, and another who belonged to the same party said that they were quite different. We flew through the tropical clouds of a turbulent dawn, below forest-covered mountain peaks, and then out across the flat coastal plantations.

La Ceiba, suddenly, was no longer a Spanish American town. It belonged to the West Indies. A midget steam engine with a huge funnel and a ridiculous toot came panting up the street pulling a train of bananas. There were donkeys tethered to wooden verandas, and no Indians at all. I left my bag at the Hotel de los Angeles and went to look for the promised boat to Guanaja.

There was, indeed, a steamer tied to the end of the jetty, but she was loading bananas and was going to take them to Hamburg. Then I saw another boat, the size of a small fishing-boat, moored half under the pier. It was called the *Sally Jones*, and on the deck, under an awning, was a swarthy man eating rice. I shouted down to him. Yes, he said, between mouthfuls, they were going to sail in about an hour, when the skipper came back from ashore, but they weren't going to Guanaja. Were they going to Roatán, then, or to any of the other islands? No, they were going along to Trujillo, and then down the Mosquito Coast. A ten day trip. It seemed that I had the choice of spending the weekend in La Ceiba or rolling for the next ten days along the coast of Central America in the *Sally Jones*. The skipper, when he came, was no more helpful.

106

'The *Patricia* would have taken you, but she's gone now,' he said.

'The *Patricia* gone?' asked the man eating rice. 'Where she gone to?'

'Didn't you hear? She sunk.'

'She sunk?'

'Yeh, she's on the bottom.'

'Jesus Christ. Poor bloody *Patricia*.'

'Yeh, poor bloody *Patricia*.'

The *Patricia*, the skipper told us, had moored alongside the jetty at Puerto Cortés, and the crew had got quietly drunk in the cabin. When they woke up the water was coming in and the boat was already settling on the bottom. Someone had left a sea-cock open. Poor bloody *Patricia*.

Another voice shouted from somewhere.

'How about Utila?'

I looked to see where it came from. Moored between two piles of the pier was a boat, a sort of half-breed between a dugout canoe and a racing eight, containing a small engine at one end and two boys, a white one and a black one, at the other. The white boy was looking at me.

'How about coming to Utila?'

'Where's that?'

'There,' he said, pointing out to sea. I looked, but I could see nothing.

'How far?'

'Twenty miles. We're off now, before the wind gets up.'

'Come on,' said the black boy. 'Let's go, before it gets up.' I fetched my bag, and we set off.

Very soon I found myself singing hymns. Butterflies started off with us, flying unsteadily over the sea, but as the wind increased they were blown away. The boat was designed for neither buoyancy nor stability, and the steep brisk seas soon filled it up; the little waves rocked it like a tub and slopped over the gunwale, and the bigger ones burst on my back and collapsed inboard. The white boy, sitting on the engine with the tiller strings in his hands and his eyes

107

screwed up against the waves, drove the boat as if we were in a race—which I rather think we were, for the wind got steadily stronger and the seas bigger—and the black boy, for three hours without stopping, baled the water out. They both shouted above the wind and the roar of the engine, and I sang.

'O God our help in ages past . . . Watch out ! . . . We'll soon get to the roughest bit . . . Christ, look at this one . . . Time like an ever-rolling stream . . . Eh? . . . Bears all its . . . How about a cigarette? . . . sons away . . . They're all wet through . . . There, look at the colour now, it's shallower, so it's rougher . . . They fly forgotten . . . We're out of gas ! . . . as a dream . . . Pass that can, will you? . . . Dies at the opening day . . . Poor bloody *Patricia* . . . We're nearly half-way now . . . Watch out ! '

I was so resigned to being drowned that it came almost as a disappointment when the butterflies began to appear again. A tiny blob on the horizon ahead spread whiskers to each side and turned into palm trees, cottages, a white church and a hill. I was put ashore on a little wooden jetty leading to a two-storeyed house with a veranda. My clothes and all my baggage were drenched, I was miserably cold, my eyes were stinging with salt, and, final irony, I was bitterly sunburnt. Stunned and shivering, I walked up the jetty to the house. On the veranda, lying in a hammock, was an old woman with the sort of wrinkled face that appears on calendars of rural England. She was called Mrs. Wilson.

'We're British,' she said, after I had had a shower in an outhouse and a meal of rice and black beans and ginger-bread. 'That's all there is to it. We're British.'

She was dead right. I had landed in a village stretched along the shore of a tiny Caribbean island, backed by palm trees and inhabited by a community of men and women and children who were still, to all appearances, living deep in the English countryside, suspended somewhere in the middle of the nineteenth century. I stayed with them for three days.

The first Englishmen to occupy the Bay Islands had been pirates who lay in wait for the Spanish ships coming out of Honduran and Guatemalan harbours, and a few of the present inhabitants are descended from them. But the first settlers, Samuel Warren and William Cooper, arrived in the 1830s; the Cooper family is now the biggest on Utila. Later settlers came from Barbados, or the Cayman Islands, or direct from England; their descendants are interested in their ancestry and proud of their pedigrees. 'My grandmother was Irish,' said old Mrs. Wilson. 'She was born in Key West when her parents were on their way out.' About a quarter of the population is negro, but the rest is pure white, and it is difficult to believe that they have never been to England; neither had their fathers nor, in many cases, their grandfathers.

'Only an Englishman would come over in a dory in a sea like that,' said Clarence Rose, an old man with a smooth pink face and a weak heart. 'I knew you were an Englishman even before you landed.' He had never been further than British Honduras in his life, but he welcomed me as a compatriot.

As I walked down the village that first evening old men touched their caps and said, 'Evening, sir,' and boys looked up cheerily and said, 'Hello.' Bucolic English villagers stood chatting under the mango trees, plump girls in flowery cotton frocks sat in rocking-chairs outside their cottages, and skinny girls pedalled slowly along the path on old Hercules bicycles; wheelbarrows and boats and a few ponies are the only other transport they have on Utila. A bare-foot child with fair pigtails ran out from under the bread-fruit trees yelling, 'Mum-mmeee!' and a great bosomy woman scooped it up and kissed it better. When she put it down again it ran off shouting, 'You can't catch *me*!' and a piccaninny the colour of a black currant with huge birdlike eyes dashed out after it.

The houses, built of wood weathered to a pretty grey and perched on stilts, had sash windows, deep eaves and shady verandas. Inside was a glimpse of polished furniture, an ancient wireless, a dresser with a clock and a china dog. Outside were creepers of neatly trimmed bougainvillaea, but if you shut your eyes you could smell lavender and honeysuckle. Even the underclothes hanging on the line—long limbs blown out and bouncing in the wind—could only be English.

'We have no apple orchards or pear trees,' said a young man

sadly, who could never have seen either. But they do have horseflies and dragonflies mingling with the humming-birds and pelicans to remind the traveller, if not the villagers, of an English summer's day, and there are other traditions which the climate cannot take away, such as the Saturday night dance and the Sunday morning hangover. At night I lay in Mrs. Wilson's white-washed guest-room, on a brass bed with a feather mattress, and listened to the rustle of the palms, the lapping on the beach, and the pips of the B.B.C. time signal.

The village church is the Methodist, with an English minister, and most of the villagers belong to it, but there are three other chapels—a Baptist, a Seventh Day Adventist and a Church of God —all with local preachers. Early on Sunday morning I was woken by a shrill chapel bell ringing through the coconut palms, and very soon the whole village was singing hymns. All four chapels were going full belt, grown-ups in two of them and Sunday school in the other two; in one of them the congregation was singing 'The old grey mare she ain't what she used to be,' with a thin-faced woman punching out the tune on an old cottage piano. And then came the procession home, the women in front carrying parasols, the men behind, brushing the dust off their best suits, and two or three luscious negresses in pink dresses, with their hair in ringlets and chattering in faintly Devonshire accents.

I could never understand the villagers when they talked among themselves, but when they spoke to me they used an accent which seemed to be a mixture of West Country and American. Many of the young men go to the United States to work in the docks or as Mississippi river pilots, and some of them retire to Utila, though the successful ones never come back. There are village boys who have become lawyers and doctors in the States, and the most distinguished of them all is a Vice-Admiral in the American navy. Old Clarence Rose keeps track of them all.

'We've got six hundred and thirty males and six hundred and seventy females. That's why we have a few virgins and no homosexuals.' About a hundred of the men work in the banana boats of The Company, and there is anxiety in the village about the state of the Honduras banana business and the rumours of ships being laid up.

The islanders who remain on Utila lead a far more idle life than villagers anywhere in England. Some of them have little plantations, or make extra money by selling fish in La Ceiba; there is a small trade in dried fish, which they keep and sell to the Catholic mainland during Lent, cherishing a mild belief that perhaps these Roman superstitions were designed so that good god-fearing folk can find a profitable market. 'And who knows,' said the Methodist minister, 'if it's not somewhere in the gift of Providence to create such a situation?'

But life in Utila, he told me, is not as innocent as it seems. On New Year's Eve, for instance, when his church was crammed full, and there were more people outside joining in the service, a thief went and raided one of the village shops, the property of the mayor, who was a very popular man. The culprit was discovered, but nothing ever happened to him; it's not difficult to buy your way out of a Honduras prison. And on the same night, while the owner was in church, a plantation was set on fire and destroyed out of spite and vindictiveness.

'What we need,' said the minister, 'is an ordinary English country bobby. He'd do wonders.' I was quite surprised to learn that there wasn't one.

A few weeks before I went there, the Comandante of Utila, who was half an islander and half a Hondureño, shot and killed a man. He had already, previously, shot another man in the leg, and a woman in the foot, and then one day, in an argument with a drunken negro, he pulled out his pistol and shot him in the stomach. The victim was taken by boat across to La Ceiba, but they couldn't save him, and his body was brought back for a martyr's funeral. Feeling in the village ran high, but there was nobody to arrest the Comandante, and he threatened to shoot his way out if anybody came to take him. As the funeral procession marched down the village, the coffin draped with the Honduras flag and the minister out in front, the murderer came to the veranda of the Comandancia, waving his pistols and roaring with laughter. He remained for

111

several days, but eventually he was taken away, though nobody really expected him to be punished.

'Of course,' said Clarence Rose, 'it was his Spanish blood.'

For the most part, however, life on Utila is unexciting. The climate is too hot for anyone to feel very energetic, and the island grows just enough for the inhabitants to live on; Castro is about as real a threat as Old Boney. For anyone with ambitions there is a monthly boat to British Honduras, and from there it is not hard to get to the United States. Those who remain constitute a curious and attractive phenomenon—partly an English country village, partly a native settlement on a Caribbean island. They are not colonial settlers, they have no club, and they will never have any home leave, but though their roots are among the palms and mango trees they have preserved an atavistic nostalgia for the England they have never seen. At night they go into their houses, change into slippers, switch on the wireless and tune in to the B.B.C.

The only foreigner is an old Dane known in the village as Uncle John. He retired to Utila after a life prospecting for oil in Venezuela, and when he arrived he started a Boy Scouts troop, adopted one of the village boys, and organized the building of a canal through the island, so that canoes could get to the fishing-grounds on the other side without risking the open sea. He was astonished that nobody had ever done it before. But soon he too succumbed to the insidious local indifference and idleness, and now he writes memoirs and histories that are never published.

On my last afternoon I met an old cottager with his braces outside his faded blue shirt and white whiskers showing under his Panama hat. He was leaning against a post, one hand clutching the rheumatism in his back, and I stopped to talk to him. He might have been a gardener in a Berkshire rectory a hundred years ago, and it was hard to believe that those pale blue eyes had never seen a pint of mild. He had spent his life working in a dry-dock in New Orleans.

'You take my advice, sir,' he said, noticing my sun-blistered face. 'Get yourself a hat, sir, get yourself a hat.' Then suddenly he

112

straightened up, wrinkled his white eyebrows, and said, 'Tell me, sir. How's Churchill?'

*   *   *

The Maya ruins at Copán are infinitely more beautiful than those at Tikal, in Guatemala. Magnificent pyramids stand on the cropped grass, as if in a park, with huge trees and a quiet, peaceful, tended atmosphere; stone *stelae* are scattered around haphazardly, like silent, wondering people. There are yellow and orange birds, and birds with long tails and Roman beaks, and birds that fly slowly past your face, slightly outraged, and birds that sit and laugh aloud at you. In the ball court there are butterflies dancing through the hot air, stupefied. A great grey animal with a long tail and a long snout slips over the old stones and dissolves into the forest.

*   *   *

San Pedro Sula is the commercial centre of Honduras, the capital of the prosperous, expanding north, close to the ports and the banana plantations. It faces the Caribbean, the United States, the world—and has its back on Tegucigalpa, which it considers effete and rather boring. Much of the local business is in the tight fists of a tight little society of *turcos*, mostly Palestinians, Lebanese and Christian Arabs. Some of them used to send money to Nasser, but on the whole they keep everything to themselves. A few Englishmen sit behind the mosquito gauze of their verandas, drinking whisky and talking about women, Mozart, business. There is an inevitable Dutchman, building a bridge or working for a shipping agent; the sweat pours down his back, trickles down his forearms, soaks into the waist-band of his trousers, so he goes on drinking. There is a Japanese too: 'Good market, but they do not understand business here, they are not businessmen.'

The loss of business with Cuba is badly felt. Cuba, being one of the most prosperous countries in the neighbourhood, but possessing no forests of her own, used to be the biggest customer for

113

Honduras timber; but now the logs are piling up. The local attitude is, 'Poor Cuba, she's lost. Lovable, erratic Cuba, the most brilliant child in the class, but so hopeless! She never could do the right thing. Poor Cuba!'

Honduras is doing something about it; roads are being built and streets surfaced. But it is all terribly, dangerously slow. About as slow as the long funeral processions that seem always to be marching through the dust of San Pedro Sula, past the ever-building, never-finished cathedral. The men march in front, sheepish and self-conscious, and the women follow in black veils; behind comes a stream of cars and trucks smothered with wreaths. A man dashes from the procession and into a café: 'Quick, a coffee! Quick!'

Corruption, as everybody admits, is the trouble. It's the biggest obstacle for the country's development, and all the bigger for not being considered dishonest. Every official takes his cut, and he would be counted not only a fool if he didn't, but a bad official also. His commission is part of his salary.

A few miles from San Pedro Sula is La Lima, the headquarters of The Company—The United Fruit Company of Boston. At La Lima the few people who ever think of Castro only think of him as a jackanapes, or a joke. The manager, a shiny man with sad eyes, sat in an office surrounded by photographs of distinguished visitors, early directors and old-fashioned steamers with tall funnels. Sorrowfully, almost apologetically, he explained that the gross profits had fallen in ten years from 314 million dollars to only 304 million. He was proud of the schools, hospitals, ports, railways that The Company had built in Honduras, and which benefited many more people than just The Company's employees; he was proud too of the dividends. The Company had done it all. Without The Company Honduras would be nowhere.

But now The Company was drawing in its horns. Terrible damage had been done to the banana plantations by a hurricane in 1954, followed by floods, labour troubles and Panama disease. Then unexpected competition had come from Ecuador, where small-scale planters were producing bananas that were cheaper and also immune to the disease. The Company had handed their railway over to the government, and was now trying to hand the hospital over as well. But the government didn't want it; it wanted to go on benefiting from The Company's hospital without the burden of running it. It had no conscience, no shame and no desire for responsibility; no patriotism either. Nobody in Honduras had much patriotism these days; the only people who worked loyally and unselfishly were the employees of The Company.

The manager was not angered so much as bewildered and saddened. The climate had melted and mellowed his feelings. Honduras was ungrateful, and The Company, the glorious, efficient, colossal successful Company, which had never meant any harm to anyone, which had only tried to do its best for the shareholders, and which was the finest, proudest, biggest, richest banana Company in the world, was beginning to tremble.

In the spacious outer office the clerks gently working at their ledgers were scarcely reached by the huge languid fans flapping from the ceiling. The clerks and the fans both seemed to be slowly stopping. The Company was like an old dog, paid off but not yet put down.

We went over to The Company's club, where the rattle of dice from a party of employees mocked the rows of empty tables. Beyond the mosquito gauze lay the vivid grass and red flags of The Company golf course, the best in the country. Everything at La Lima is the best in the country. And beyond the golf course stretched the bananas, miles and miles and miles of them.

VI

Nicaragua

IN LONDON I FOUND THE NICARAGUAN CONSULATE in a narrow street near Oxford Circus, at the top of a tall and shabby house. The staircase got cobwebbier and cobwebbier as I climbed it, but at last I reached a tiny attic filled with filing cabinets and lined with calendars and typed regulations. At the only table, defended by a mountain of files, bills of lading and rubber stamps, sat a little old man with a foxy face and rimless spectacles, like a frightened animal caught in a hole. He moved in little swift darts, jabbing at a signature, tearing at a piece of paper, dashing for another file. Eventually he gave me a visa.

That same afternoon I went to the Costa Rican consulate in South Kensington. Pushing open the double doors of a huge mansion I walked into a drawing-room whose walls were decorated with acres of gold-framed mirrors and vast oil paintings. The polished parquet floor was almost bare, but in the middle, under a chandelier, was a solitary table. Behind it sat the same little man.

When he had given me another visa I told him that next morning I should be applying for one at the Guatemalan consulate. Perhaps, I suggested, we might meet again. He took off his spectacles, and looked thoughtfully up at the moulded cornice. 'Guatemala?' he said, as if trying to picture it. 'Guatemala? Ah, no. But there . . . there you will find my wife.'

But if the two republics share a visa clerk in London, and a frontier in Central America, they have very little else in common.

Managua, the capital of Nicaragua, was destroyed by an earth-quake thirty years ago, and one may wonder why they ever built it up again. It is on the shores of Lake Managua, but that is nothing to recommend it, for acrid smells creep up into the streets, the water

116

is brown and wind-lashed, and, except for a volcano on the far side, it is not a pretty lake.

The most attractive feature of Managua is the habit its people have, in the evening, of bringing their rocking-chairs out on to the pavement. It is impossible to walk more than a few yards down a street, for at almost every front door one is stopped by a family circle, all bobbing up and down in their chairs, and forcing one to step out into the traffic. But one doesn't complain, for it is a friendly and aesthetic custom. Sometimes, out of discretion, the family sits in the inner, palm-filled patio, or round the parlour television set, while the only members in the cool of the street are a young man and his girl, rocking silently in unison and touching fingers across the arms of their chairs.

The heat in Managua is devastating. It's more than just a matter of temperature, it's another element—a hot liquid clinging to you, encasing you, through which you have to move. It moulds your face, slips down your shirt, chokes in your throat, smothers you; and if there's a wind it doesn't cool you, but merely presses the heat harder against you. When you lift your hand the heat brushes past it as though you were lifting it through water, and you look down to see if the flesh has shrivelled, or cooked a little. You are plunged into it, and broiled alive. The sweat pours from your forehead and stings in your eyes, trickles into your mouth, under your chin, behind your ears, down the back of your head. And suddenly it turns cold on your back, so that you shiver as you sweat.

The coolest thing I saw in Managua was a troop of nuns, in heavy black robes with their cowls tight round their cheeks and across their foreheads; they must have been filled with an inner, lasting coolness. An American in a transparent Hawaiian shirt that showed his nipples was infinitely hotter.

The second curse of Managua is dust. It blows down the streets, and settles everywhere; in the morning you have to brush it off your pillow. The answer is air-conditioning; but personally I prefer to be hot, to sweat, and even to smell. Living in an air-conditioned room is like sitting in a cinema and watching the tropics on the screen.

I went into the Librería Americana, hoping for a paperback novel, but there wasn't a book in sight; the shop seemed to be filled with children's tricycles. In the Librería Nicaragüense I was luckier, but most of the books were about gynaecology and birth control—which perhaps explained the children's tricycles.

On all the lamp posts, on the statues of the national heroes, and even pasted along the pavement curbs, were advertisements for the film of *Ben-Hur*. Somewhere Bing Crosby growled through the fetid heat. An American said, 'Something'll have to be done about that guy Castro, that's for sure.' An old English lady who had come out as a child in 1898 said, 'Oh yes, we had fun riding up to the coffee plantations in ox-wagons; we had fun in those wagons.' And a grey-haired man who might have been a school-master came up to me: 'Good morning, Mr. Wollaston. Change dollars?' I had been in the country about an hour.

*   *   *

Nicaragua is a dictatorship, or rather, as the cynics of Managua say, it is ruled by a dynasty. Between 1936 and 1956 the reigning President was General Anastasio Somoza, and on his assassination he was succeeded by his elder son, Luís, while his younger son took command of the army. The Somozas run the country as a family business, allowing nobody else to interfere, and they undoubtedly make substantial profits for the shareholders. But dividends denote successful business, and the company, Nicaragua, is by no means grinding to a halt. However, as with all family businesses, the directors are convinced that nobody else could run it as well as they do. And they are probably quite right.

It would be surprising, of course, if there were no Nicaraguans who were in favour of nationalizing the firm, and there are indeed many of them—patriotic young men, fanatical about democracy, deeply concerned about events in other parts of Latin America, and sickened by the sight of the bulging Somoza coffers. There is also a large number of people, not quite so high-minded, who are equally sickened at those coffers, but only because they feel that

118

the Somozas have been in the board-room for long enough, and that now it's somebody else's turn. Far down below these groups, grumbling away in the workers' canteen, are the Fidelistas.

For them, Castro is the man who has brought land reform, broken the rule of the rich, laughed at the United States, and above all produced something new. A few months before I arrived in Nicaragua they had got so rowdy that Somoza had had to lock up a couple of hundred of them, and Managua was officially declared to be in a state of siege. But they know that, so long as Castro remains a dirty word, everything is on their side, and that unless the patriotic young men who are the only people in the country with a genuine social conscience, can organize themselves pretty quickly, it will soon be too late.

Even if Castro has lost a little favour through his final surrender to communism and his suppression of liberty, he still has wide, though inarticulate, sympathy in Central America. He may have antagonized some people by his attack on the Church, but the influence of the Church seems an exaggerated factor. They were never the most liberal, nor the most Christian, people who leaned towards me in an argument and pulled out the stale old plum: 'You see, this is a *Catholic* country.'

In Nicaragua the political opposition is divided among no less than seven different parties, of whom the two chief ones both call themselves Conservatives—the Nicaraguan Conservative Party, and the Conservative Party of Nicaragua. The leader of one of them is a doctor, and he gave me a bundle of pamphlets and told me how his party was the true democratic opposition, with a policy of justice and reform, and that the other Conservative party was merely a bunch of greedy capitalists and land-owners who were after the perks of government. The leader of the other Conservative party, a lawyer, gave me a bundle of almost identical pamphlets and told me the same story. They both insisted that the biggest problem for Nicaragua was to get rid of the Somoza family; once that was done, the country could go ahead. But when I suggested that they might unite to bring down the dynasty they were aghast; they had far nastier things to say about each other than about even President Somoza.

However, all is not desolation. There is a Nicaraguan newspaper edited by a dedicated young man who, like the two Conservative party leaders, knows instinctively what is needed, but whereas they have no will and almost no intention of doing anything about it, he has both. He sees that democracy means nothing without education; that because democracy means government by the people, the people must consciously want it; and that what they want first is houses, health, jobs, security and a leader they can identify themselves with. They can't with Somoza; they can with Castro.

The United States, he said, held the key. It should show a new heart, and the people of Latin America were desperately anxious for it to do so; but even though the Kennedy administration had raised such hopes—hopes based perhaps more on needs than on realities—there hadn't been many signs of any new attitudes. The right-wing dictators ought to be as much anathema as the left-wing ones, but the United States couldn't be persuaded to take much interest in Nicaragua; in Cuba, on the other hand, where a thousand million dollars had gone down the drain, it was different, and the world had watched the tragic, shameful spectacle of an American-sponsored invasion. The final insult to this earnest, patriotic man, was that part of the invasion had set out from Nicaraguan soil.

But he was muzzled. For the past six months, and at several other times during the Somoza dynasty, there had been a government censor at work in the office of his paper, and every day the best bits were snipped out. What was the use of having a paper, he cried, if he couldn't write that more than three hundred different properties in Managua province alone belonged to members of the Somoza family, as well as the state shipping line, the airline, the Mercedes Benz agency and untold other businesses? And if for years his photographers had taken pictures of President Somoza always with the American ambassador at his elbow—an ambassador whose constant visits to the palace and whose role as unofficial godfather to the ruling family had done nothing to dispel a general belief in American approval of the regime—how could he ever persuade his

120

readers that a new ambassador sent by a new administration in Washington marked a new deal, when nothing else in the United States' behaviour towards Latin America seemed to have altered at all?

*   *   *

'You must make allowances for the Latin Americans,' they say. But I really don't see why you should. They don't make any allowances for themselves—they are often haughty and contemptuous, and alarmingly antagonized by criticism. As I travelled through Central America I began to wonder what the people there had been doing all these years. Considering the vigour and the bravery of the conquistadors and the speed at which the Spanish colonies were settled, it is astonishing that after about the end of the sixteenth century nothing happened at all. Intermarriage and the climate dulled the zeal and stifled the imagination of the descendants of some of the most energetic people in history.

Now, at last, something has happened. A new idea has arrived in their world, and they are beginning to bother.

'What is it in communism that people find so attractive?' asked an old businessman in Managua. 'What is it? I wish I knew. When I went to the States even quite intelligent people were talking about it. What's it all about? What do the communists want? Hasn't that fellow Khruschev got enough to worry about without bothering us?'

I asked him to tell me what he really thought about Nicaraguan politics and the Somoza regime, but he became vague and apologetic. 'I can't say. I live here, you see. I have to think of my business. I must make money.'

*   *   *

I met the colonel at a bar, a huge man with a huge stomach, sitting on a stool, filling himself with beer and letting it seep out through his skin, like a leaky barrel. After years of filling the barrel

121

you might think that the cracks would have tightened up, but the beer still came pouring out, and he had to be constantly pouring in more.

'You like our beer?' he asked. He couldn't possibly be a Nicaraguan—he had more energy than any Nicaraguan could dream of—and between bottles of beer I learnt that he was a Hungarian. He had been in Nicaragua nearly thirty years, apart from spells serving with the French Foreign Legion and under the flags of Britain, Israel, Costa Rica and Nicaragua. Now he was running a chemist's shop with his Nicaraguan wife, and working for a French news agency.

'Look, I will tell you,' he said confidentially, after we had had a lot of beer. 'There is tragedy in my life. You see, I loff black women. But each time I am married, I am married with a white woman. That is my tragedy. And I am too the victim of academic women. My first wife was a Mexican, a doctor of medicine. This one is a Nicaraguan, a doctor of pharmacy. Yes, I am victim. And I loff black women.'

On Nicaraguans he was scathing. 'There are two kinds, the rich and the poor. But they both are lazy. It's because of *mestizaje*. Do you know *mestizaje*? It's intermarrying with the Indians, that's the trouble. And with the blacks; but that's . . . that's different. I'm not a racist, but just look around! Who are the big names? They are not Nicaraguans, apart from Somoza—and he's a fine man, a real man, you will like him. No, they are Russians, Jews, even English. Ha! There are two brothers, the Moncrieff-Chamberlains—Reginaldo and Archibaldo. What do you think of that? Very aristocratic, yes? They were born in Nicaragua, but of course they are English. And me, I'm a Hungarian. It's easy for us to do well, and make money. That's the trouble with the Nicaraguans—*mestizaje*.'

He roared, chuckled, waved his arms about, and drank more beer. He never finished a glass before pouring in another bottle. In his youth he had enrolled in nine different universities, but he had never got through the first term of any of them. Suddenly he bellowed like a wild animal, scooped me up in a great bear hug and carried me off into the street. Outside, a taxi was passing, and

122

without stopping it the colonel burst through the door and sat down. The driver, who didn't have to ask where we were going, who didn't in fact even stop his car to see who had got in, took us to the colonel's chemist's shop behind the market, where we sat and sweated while the colonel's wife sold aspirins and chewing-gum.

'I am an exhibitionist,' bellowed the colonel, producing his press cuttings book, and explaining how he was constantly growing a beard and then marching out and collecting a few dozen people in the streets and leading them off to a barber in the market, for the pleasure of having them watch it being shaved off. In the book were articles he had written for the local press ('I invent the news when there isn't any'), articles about obscure historical characters illustrated with old photos ('any old photo will do—I can find a grandfather for anybody'), articles defending Chiang Kai-Shek ('he's rotten, but I do it for money'). He brought out his gun from behind the jars of medicines, and a pistol from his pocket. 'Everybody knows I carry a gun, everybody. I am *respected*. I can go anywhere. At night people cross the street to keep away from me. Yes, I am *respected*. Sometimes . . . sometimes I have to shoot. In Managua it is necessary.'

He was like a conductor stirring up an orchestra. In one huge movement he leapt up, shut up the shop, seized me and his wife, carried us through the streets and pushed us, crammed us into his little house. It was already full, with trophies from his wars, archaeological books, huge chunks of stone dug up in remote corners of Nicaragua, relics from his days of soldiering under five different flags, his seventeen medals, his Légion d'Honneur, his Croix de Guerre, his old tin hat, his sword, a portrait of Beethoven by a Mexican artist making him look like an Aztec, macabre paintings of Valkyries and goddesses. But even the trophies were outnumbered by portraits of the colonel himself, in the uniform of a légionnaire with a little beard on his chin and a salacious look in his eye.

'Most people would buy a car, but I like other things. Look, this is supposed to be the garage, and I fill it with books.' There were rare books about Nicaragua, books the colonel had written, books

123

about Lawrence of Arabia, naughty French novels—all bound in leather and deep in Managua dust. Pieces of paper marked every page where the colonel, or any member of his family, was mentioned.

We drank jugs of whisky, while his wife sat at another table with a newspaper and the colonel told me stories of the wars he had fought and the women he had loved. Somewhere, in a dark corner of the room, a baby was asleep in a cot.

Again he scooped me up, and without a word to his wife carried me off to a restaurant where we sat at a pavement table drinking more beer and eating rice and squid. 'This is the Bohemia of Nicaragua,' roared the colonel, and it was full of fat, laughing young men, from newspapers and radio stations. Though they were mostly much younger than the colonel they all had bellies to match his, hanging over the fronts of their chairs; as they laughed their bellies wobbled, and the vibrations made them laugh all the more.

There was a drunken negro who said he was Castro's enemy number one, and wrote a letter for me to take back to Cuba for Castro, but the colonel grabbed it and threw it in the gutter. The proprietor was a little old Spaniard from the Canary Islands who had been exiled years ago from Costa Rica and had grown beyond taking any interest in the affairs of his boisterous customers—affairs of rebellion, feud and filibustering.

'I am a soldier,' said the colonel. 'I loff to fight. I am getting again restless. I am looking for a war. Do you know where I can fight?' Then he leaned forward: 'And there is also my tragedy. You see, I loff black women.'

*   *   *

Most people don't complain at all. The *status quo* is their only criterion, and they have nothing to complain about because they have nothing to compare it with. But some people—a very few—do complain.

'I'm not an anti-American,' they say, 'but . . .' and they plunge into a torrent of anti-Americanism. The U.S. Marine Corps finally

124

left Nicaragua nearly thirty years ago, after an intermittent and hated occupation, but the memory is still strong enough to colour people's opinions of present-day Americans. They don't bother to learn Spanish, they don't mix with Nicaraguans, they don't even talk to them at the bar of the country club or play a round of golf with them, they get all their food flown up specially from the Panama Canal Zone, the ambassador follows President Somoza around like a puppy. Americans are personally disliked, which is worse than any political disapproval.

Other people complain about corruption. They complain about the business practices of men who are otherwise respected, reputable, responsible members of society, and whose wives go regularly to church. A man buys a new car, on which an import duty is to be paid; but he gets it imported in the name of a friend, a senior army officer who doesn't have to pay the duty, in consideration for a small present. Who loses? The people who are starving in the streets, perhaps, but that is somebody else's affair, and everybody knows that anyway the tax would never have got further than some official's pocket. The man is proud of his car, but even more proud of his skill at avoiding the tax, and proudest still of being a friend of such a clever, high-up officer. And besides, it's a joke—something to laugh about as well as swank about.

People complain about legal justice—about its absence. A woman whose husband and children were murdered saw the convicted murderer a few months later, sitting with his friends in a café; his father had bought his release from prison. Imprisonment can mean anything; some prisoners are tortured, others are feasted by their jailers. The length of a term in prison doesn't depend on the crime, or even on the sentence of the court, but on the prisoner's connections, and his value. And for those whose existence, in prison or at large, is just too embarrassing for the government, there is always the *Ley de Fuga*—'shot while attempting to escape.'

People in Managua, on the west side of Nicaragua, complain about the comparative prosperity of the Caribbean coast, where the banana plantations and mahogany forests are. Until air travel joined them to the capital, the ports of Bluefields, Greytown and Puerto

Cabezas belonged almost to a different country, and the laughing negroes who come from that part complain about the apathy of the people of Managua. 'Who ever heard of one of us who'd just sit and suffer?' said a black beauty in an office.

But the biggest complaint is about the Somozas. Everyone knows that without the ruling family Nicaragua would be nothing—and the knowledge is enough to vex anybody with pride, ambition or merely sensitivity, who cannot claim even to be the most distant cousin.

*   *   *

I had never met a dictator before, and although I had been warned that President Somoza was not the kind with horns who eat babies for breakfast I wasn't prepared for the amiable young man who received me. The appointment was for seven in the evening, but I had to wait for an hour and twenty minutes in an air-conditioned waiting-room of the palace before I was called in; I had been warned about that too, for the President, who is both chairman and managing director of the firm, is a very busy man.

Also in the waiting-room sat three other visitors, and we all tried to appear as cool and nonchalant as we felt, only occasionally drumming the back of an empty chair with our fingers, or tapping a squeaky shoe on the floor, or picking a nose. At a desk in one corner sat a tiny army officer, cubic in shape, with an enormous gold wrist watch, a gold ballpoint pen, several gold rings on his sleeves, a pistol in his belt and a telephone far out of his reach. Other, lesser soldiers came in and out, with similar watches and pens and pistols, but fewer rings on their sleeves. When the telephone rang, one of them would hand the receiver to the little officer, who dropped into a brief, cryptic conversation; and when he wanted to make a call he leaned across the big desk and flicked the dial with his gold ballpoint pen. Once his hand went to his pistol, and I thought he was going to flick the dial with the muzzle, or even shoot at the numbers he wanted, but suddenly he remembered, or else changed his mind, and pulled out the pen instead.

A door opened and the President's press secretary called me in. I found myself in a huge room with a long table surrounded by chairs, at the far end of which sat the dictator. In Central America one doesn't often see pictures of the local boss, perhaps because of his often ephemeral nature, and in fact the only faces well-known to everybody are those of the Virgin Mary and Castro; but I had memorized the features of Somoza for fear of blurting out my first well-rehearsed words to the wrong man, and there was no mistaking him—fat and faintly pig-like, with protruding ears, little eyes and a gold chain round his wrist. He got up and walked towards me with his hand out. 'How kind of you, Mr. Wollaston . . .' and we sat down, he at the end of the table, me on his right and the press secretary on his left.

Suddenly there was a flash, and I realized that a photographer had followed me in. On the table in front of us were a telephone, a box of cigarettes, a packet of chewing-gum and a vast heap of papers. For an hour, although it was late at night and he clearly had a lot of business to finish, the President told me about his country.

The more he talked the more I began to think less of a tycoon running a gigantic private business than of a proud, benign and thrifty farmer, who knew his land better than anyone else, and who was working it efficiently and developing it with devotion. The figures were all in his head, his arguments were lucid and impressive, he never lapsed into swank or false modesty; he was enlightened, wise, patriotic, modern, and without rancour or arrogance. Definitely a gentleman farmer. Should the farm animals have any say in the management? Why ever?

The Tweedledum and Tweedledee of the two Conservative parties, when I asked them what was the most pressing need for Nicaragua, had both replied, 'To bring down the Somozas.' But President Somoza himself—and I nearly stood up and cheered— said simply, 'Education.' Without education there was little hope of increasing productivity, and none at all for democracy.

Integration of the six Central American republics, which had been talked about spasmodically for years, was another of his favourite hobby-horses, and he did not seem unwilling to contribute his own country to a federation. With economic integration would come the gradual smoothing of frontier problems, the lessening of controls, the standardization of currency, and eventual political integration—'in seventy or eighty years, perhaps.' It was comforting to hear a man talk about such a distant future with such confidence. So far, he said, it was only the bigger capitalists who opposed integration, but very soon they would see the advantages; the federation would have a population of nearly ten million, which constituted a decent-sized market, and outside investment would easily be attracted. Hitherto foreign investors had robbed the country of its resources, but now they must be encouraged to develop local manufacturing and light industries, to increase the standard of living, which in turn would increase the value of the market.

To nationalize industry, however, was going too far. 'Our Latin American governments are no good at running businesses'—and the President smiled the same smile that a farmer might put on if you suggested that his cowman should get a commission on the herd's milk production.

His view extended beyond his own frontier: 'The Caribbean is the melting-pot of America; we had the first independent republic after the United States, and now we have the first communist one.' He was sympathetic with Washington's alarm: 'They simply can't afford to have a communist country only ninety miles away, with Russian missiles and all that; if it was Argentina, or Chile, it would be different, but Cuba is too close.' He was sensational about the threat of subversion: 'One day we found a Czech—imagine, a Czech!—walking along the beach, on our Caribbean coast; he said he was a sailor on his way from Honduras to Costa Rica, to pick up a new ship. These are the people who help our communists and Fidelistas.' He was bothered by the Cuban revolution, not only as a threat: 'I don't understand why it should have been the Cubans. They are all so individualistic, and they had the highest standard of living in Latin America.' He was confident that more liberal countries of Latin America were on the right lines: 'Look at Mexico! It's not yet industrialized, but already it's got beyond being just under-developed, mainly through land reform. And education—
128

that's the thing.' And finally he was sanguine about the future:
'Don't you worry too much about communism. We have plenty
of honest men—even in Latin America.'

I came away reeling, and trying to reconcile my prejudices with
a suspicion that the Nicaraguans were lucky to be in the hands of
such a capable man. To be merely the best dictator they have, when
the competition is so poor, is no great achievement, but President
Somoza is more than that. It was long past nine, and there were
more people sitting in the waiting-room. 'He works till eleven, or
twelve, or one,' said the press secretary with a yawn, and the next
day he sent me a copy of the photograph.

VII

Costa Rica

AT SAN JOSÉ, THE CAPITAL OF COSTA RICA, AN HOUR after leaving the heat of Managua, I had gooseflesh. As the aeroplane crossed the frontier between the two republics the air hostess walked slowly and symbolically down the cabin spraying us all with disinfectant. We spent half an hour circling through thick cloud and mist, then suddenly dived from a great height, skimmed over some banana trees and tore along a flooded runway, with reflected airport buildings. But the pilot thought better of it, opened the throttle and roared back into the clouds. Three more times we circled steeply, and then with another violent, stomach-tearing swoop, we landed like a duck on the tarmac.

'Like too much England,' said the man from Bogotá sitting next to me, sadly looking out at the rainswept buildings, and to emphasize the efficiency of the country we had arrived in a man came running through the rain with a bundle of black umbrellas; he stood at the door of the aeroplane opening one for each passenger, and we marched in file under them to the customs shed. It was difficult to believe that we were still in Latin America.

I found it even harder to believe it when I first walked through the streets of San José. In Nicaragua most of the people are *mestizos*, a mixture of Spanish and Indian, with a number of negroes along the Caribbean coast, but in Costa Rica, particularly up in the central highlands where three-quarters of the people live, almost the entire population is pure Spanish. San José is a European town.

'Costa Rica is certainly civilized and democratic and prosperous, and all the things that we should like to be,' a slightly embittered Nicaraguan had said, 'but it is so dull. It is the Switzerland of

Central America.' And then he added, as a malicious afterthought, 'The Costa Ricans—they have no hormones.'

I saw at once what he meant. There are almost no potholes in the streets, the pavements are much less liable to trip you up, and the buildings have an air of impeccable respectability. To judge from the shop windows, the people of San José spend their time buying watches, jewellery, plastic mackintoshes, cream cakes and Dunhill pipes; they are given to travelling, for every fourth shop seems to be an airline office, and to hypochondria, for there is an equally astonishing number of clinics. Men walk along in blue suits and homburg hats, with macs folded over their arms; elderly women in black carry umbrellas, or bunches of arum lilies, as if they were for ever on their way to a wedding or a funeral; elder sisters wear smart navy coats and skirts, and younger sisters wear white socks and flouncy frocks; and old men up from the country sell orchids.

In the Parque Central is a huge bandstand, and underneath it, not a bandsmen's green room, or a public lavatory, but a bookshop. In it, next to all the missals, I found a book by Kingsley Amis called *Jim el Afortunado*.

Earthquakes hardly ever happen, and when they do they usually fail to knock anything down. Even the volcanoes are only mildly active. Nothing very drastic happens at all. The newspapers print a number of repetitive articles about Costa Rica being the most democratic, most anti-Castro country in Latin America, but half the pages are given to social news, to announcements of concerts (*Eine Kleine Nachtmusik* in the town hall), and to photographs of pretty girls with cordial congratulations from their families ('*singular complacencia*') on reaching their fifteenth birthday. As the Nicaraguan said, it's all very Swiss.

There is indeed a delicious smell of coffee beans in the air, just to remind the traveller that he hasn't strayed into an unfashionable town in the Bernese Oberland, and to confuse things even more the posh hotel in the main street is resolutely called the Balmoral. It is true, too, that there are barefoot beggars, but they don't seem a problem—they are just rather quaint. In such a well-ordered town it is a shock to find a tattered family asleep at night on the cathedral

131

steps, and one almost wonders if they have been stationed there by the bishop; it wouldn't otherwise be an authentic Central American cathedral.

On my first evening I detected another jarring note when I heard the archaic strains of a guitar. Through a wide double door I looked into a brightly-lit hall, where a man in a white suit and a bow tie was strumming chords on a guitar, a woman at his elbow; they seemed to be singing a hymn. Stepping back to see what sort of a show it was, I read over the door, '*Templo Metodisto*'.

The biggest shock, however, was still to come. An immense negro loomed from a doorway, and brushing past me murmured, in a gentle, benevolent voice, 'Looking for anything special tonight?' The curious way he put it made me feel almost churlish in not stopping to do business with him; but I had nothing special in mind at all that night.

*　　　*　　　*

The swagger hotel. In the bar the fat men come and go, talking of their Pan American connections to Miami and Caracas. The sun and warmth of San José are reduced to low-powered electric lighting and frigid air-conditioning. Lunch is being eaten in the dusk, by faceless wraiths. Through a nylon curtain, beyond the banana palms and the haze of beer, flickers a silver fountain. Beside it stands a woman in a nylon blouse and slacks, tight-fitting across her bottom. Hormones at last!

She turns round, and it's another man. It was just the beer.

*　　　*　　　*

'It's a dull little country,' said someone in the British Embassy. 'They don't stand around looking at their feet. There's no more corruption than there is in most countries—certainly no more than in England. And nobody's very rich; there are a few people who change their Chevrolet every year, but it's never more than a Chevrolet.'

If Castro is a dirty word in Nicaragua, in Costa Rica it hardly enters the vocabulary. True, I saw a chalked-up notice, 'Fidel is a communist,' and an opposition one, 'Yankees quit Cuba!' but they were more statements of fact than outbursts of passion; with comparatively little social injustice there is little scope at the moment for a revolutionary. Costa Rica boasts the third highest literacy rate in Latin America, a well-run social security scheme and a record of constitutional, democratic government, with regular free elections that is the pride of every Costa Rican. There hasn't been a revolution for nearly fifteen years, the army was long ago disbanded, and they make do with a small Civil Guard; as every shoe-shine boy knows, there are more school teachers in the country than soldiers.

But worthiness, especially in a part of the world where it is such a rare commodity, breeds complacence, and that, instead of the threat of revolution which hovers over other Central American countries, is Costa Rica's danger. At the moment she has a conservative government—a *status quo* government whose chief characteristic, I was told by one of the few worried Costa Ricans I met, was *inmobilismo*. They have hesitated to join the four republics to the north in a Central American economic federation, and their policy of isolationism, with its hint of self-satisfaction, seems hardly farsighted; expansion of the economy, which the federation would bring, as well as diversification and industrialization, should be the aims, but the government, who see no cause for worry when everyone else in sight is in an even worse plight, is reluctant to try anything new. It is understandable that a country which is already one move ahead of its neighbours should be content to sit back and relax, but it doesn't seem to have occurred to its present leaders that some of the others may be taking a short cut.

An American economist in San José said he thought Costa Rica was staying out of the Central American federation scheme for fear of three things: the political fear of having her impeccable institutions infected by contamination with the less desirable systems of other countries; the social fear of having foreign labour immigrants tainting her own almost exclusively white population; and the economic fear of losing industry to other countries, where

133

wages were lower and where her goods could be underpriced. She didn't seem to realize that she could be the leader of them all, could help raise the others to her own standards, could create a big, stable market, and then go on to better things. No one looks beyond their nose; the old Latin American tradition of impermanence is too strong, nothing is solid, nothing lasts long, nobody has any faith.

Most of the Costa Ricans are happily unperturbed. They work moderately hard during the day, and in the evenings they go to the cinema. When the lights go down, a velvet-voiced man tells them that he hopes the film they are going to see will give them all complete satisfaction, and during the show the audience indulges in no vulgar whistles or cat-calls and only in the most restrained preliminaries of love-play. Afterwards they stop for an ice-cream soda at one of the cafés in the cathedral square before going home to bed. The Southern Cross hangs like a huge benediction above the rooftops.

The only embarrassment in Costa Rica is the answer to the reason why. If you ask a Costan Rican why his country is so very different from the other republics of Central America he will at first pretend that he doesn't quite understand, and ask you to explain in what way it seems to differ. Then he will mumble something about the system of land tenure; there are very few big landowners and most of the coffee and banana plantations are in the form of small holdings. If you press him further, he will tell you that Costa Rica is poor in minerals, which meant that the early Spanish settlers had to get down to working the land instead of hoping for quick fortunes. But you know that there is something else at the back of his mind, something perhaps to do with the nature of the population, something more personal, something that he is possibly proud of, but something he feels may vex you. You persist, and finally he will clear his throat, and say, ' Well, of course, I'm not a racist, but in Costa Rica we are white people, and . . .' and discreetly he will begin to blush.

*   *   *

One night three Costa Rican journalists took me to the opening ceremony of a new restaurant in the hills above San José. They said it was to be a tremendous occasion, with a barbecue and the press and members of the government and lots of women and even the President himself; I would meet all sorts of interesting people. We drove up a tortuous road, through the night, to a horrible neon-lighted building hung with coloured lamps and exuding juke-box music like a bad smell. But it had a wonderful view over the capital.

Inside was a bare room with a long table set for about fifty people, a juke-box and a bar. At the bar were half a dozen Americans, none of them sober, including the new proprietor, a spindly man who had left the States two months earlier for the first time in his life and been sold the restaurant for forty thousand dollars over a drink in San José. 'I jus' love it here,' he said, in between getting the Capitán, an Austrian, to translate his orders to the waiters into Spanish.

The Capitán had been hired for the evening to cook the barbecue and help launch the restaurant in proper style; a European touch is an authentic touch. He told me stories of his days fishing off the coast of California, and of how the crews used to take special castration tablets to keep them cool during the long weeks at sea.

We waited about three hours drinking whisky and getting hungrier and more bad-tempered. Nobody else arrived for the party and the juke-box boomed through an empty room until the Capitán forgot to put another nickel in it. Then the Americans started to sing, 'My Bonny lies over the Ocean', and the three Costa Rican journalists became angry with the American proprietor, irritated at the absence of any women, apologetic to me and embarrassed at the whole fiasco. At last we persuaded the Capitán to bring in the dinner, and he wheeled in a trolley of chicken and rice—enough for fifty guests; it tasted of charcoal, but most of the Americans were too drunk to eat. The proprietor shouted thickly at the waiters, but in the wrong language, a photographer staggered down the table flashing at each of us in turn, and the proprietor said, between whiskies and oaths and belches and mouthfuls of cremated chicken, 'I jus' love it here.'

135

The three journalists took me away and back down to San José. In the suburbs we stopped outside a house. 'Come in for a beer,' said one of them. I thought it was his home. He knocked on the door, a lattice opened, and a woman's face looked out. We were let in. Inside were curtained-off cubicles, with double beds and girls everywhere. A Frenchman welcomed us with a great roar, and led us to the bar. We had a beer and then drove home. It was a much nicer place than the American's new restaurant.

It is a pity that the Americans whom the Latin American public meets, and who create the American character in their own image, are often the ugly ones. Some of the officials I met, locked away behind the armed guards of their embassies, were quite different people; they were knowledgeable and sympathetic and desperately anxious to do the right thing. In Costa Rica a new American ambassador had just arrived who, so far from being another aloof businessman filling a job he had earned by his political enthusiasm at home, was a professional, young and dedicated; best of all, by his Mexican ancestry and fluent Spanish, he was almost a Latin American, and could be a significant and hopeful sign that the State Department, with a new administration, was beginning a new approach. Anxious Costa Ricans were watching him.

Another impressive American was working for the Institute of Political Education, a school housed in an old night club outside San José, with a programme of three-month courses for members of democratic liberal parties from all over Latin America. Night club into night school. It was still experimental, and dangerously fragile, but already it had attracted high-minded men from many countries. The Switzerland of Central America was showing the first shadowy symptoms of its own Geneva.

VIII

Panama

DOWN FROM THE ALPINE STERILITY OF SAN JOSÉ
to the sticky, steamy, sensuous fertility of Panama. The smell in
the streets of San José is of coffee beans; in Panama City it is of
shrimps. More so even than in Managua the air is laden; it feels its
way down your shirt, up your trouser legs, and it caresses your face.
Flocks of raucous little green parrots squabble in the streets. Old
wooden houses with carved gables and wrought-iron balconies totter
ridiculously; shiny black-skinned figures stand at the windows. The
young girls are ripe, like mangoes, succulent and luscious. You
feel that if you squeezed them the juice would run out. You long
to squeeze them.

In the old part of Panama City are dignified squares, fine churches
and big houses standing on the waterfront. It is the scene of
Panama's first paradox; the sun rises over the Pacific. But the rowdy,
philistine port is like any other—an excrescence, a tumour hanging
to the Panama Canal, with little affinity with the Republic of
Panama. You can buy a Leica, or a Pontiac, or a T-bone steak, or
a woman of any colour you fancy, but useful things like haircuts
and envelopes are hard to find.

American service patrols maunder through the murkier streets.
Some of the bars are 'restricted', and the girls in them are as idle
as the bottles on the shelves; once uncorked, the bottles sit there
for months, years, before someone has another go; sampled once or
twice, growing dustier every day, waiting on a whim; just like the
girls. Only the lottery ticket numbers chalked up on a board in
every bar are fresh every week. The beer is kept in huge refrigera-
tors, sometimes for so long that a bottle explodes and throws a
spray of glass splinters everywhere. The glasses are kept in the

E*   137 refrigerator too, and are brought out frosty to the bar, so that the beer doesn't gain one degree of unnecessary temperature.

A New Zealander was walking along a pavement on his way to a bar for a beer with me. A boy walked towards him, passed close to him and with a swift, deft swipe tore off his wrist watch. In the same movement he was on the back of a bicycle that another boy was riding down the gutter, and together they were round the corner. The New Zealander looked at his wrist; there was not a scratch, but only the mark left by the tight metal strap.

*   *   *

The New Zealander took me up in his Piper aeroplane and we flew across the Isthmus, from the Pacific to the Atlantic. Away over to the left, through the steam, was the Canal, a glimpse of ships gliding through the hills from one ocean to another; but we were not allowed to fly over the Canal Zone—it is a strip of American military territory ten miles wide, splitting the Republic of Panama.

At Colón we turned right along the north coast, to Portobelo, a pretty village at the head of a fine harbour with steep wooded headlands and Drake's Rock at the entrance, where he was buried. The old ruined fortifications were peppered with trim tin-roofed huts; even the cathedral had a tin roof, but the great treasure-house, where the gold from Peru had been stored, didn't have a roof at all. We flew on to Nombre de Dios Bay, but it hardly seemed worth sacking these days—a dismal settlement of huts and a single trading launch in the harbour, with canoes clamouring round it.

The New Zealander dived down over the San Blas Islands, so low that we could see the Indian women in their red and blue robes sitting outside their huts. Only the islands opposite the river mouths are inhabited; the Indians take their canoes up the rivers to cultivate patches of corn, coconuts and bananas, and in the evenings they return to their islands with fresh water. There is no room for the smallest vegetable patch on the islands; they are just coral dots in the sea, some of them so small and so thoroughly inhabited that they appear as little groups of huts floating on the surface. The Indians suffer terribly from intermarriage, and from whooping-cough.

But though they are proud and isolationist they are also adaptable. A raw young Indian arrives at Colón from his island and next day he is standing at the corner in a zoot suit, chewing bubble-gum with horrible skill, whistling at the girls and following the World Series. They adapt back again just as easily.

We flew back across the Isthmus, circling over the jungle to gain enough height for crossing the hills. Balboa took twelve days to reach the Pacific, and recently a party of American soldiers with radios and air-drops followed his track, and took sixteen; some of the soldiers had to be evacuated by helicopter. In the Piper aeroplane it took us about fifteen minutes. Rivers below us twisted like viscera through the jungle, and then we saw the mangroves, and then the mud. Such mud—the Pacific tide goes out leaving a wet desert etched with a tracery of water channels—a diagram of anatomy. Beyond, in the Pacific, the shrimp boats trailed their nets, stirring up a wake of brown mud.

We dropped to Old Panama, flying down through the frigate-birds and boobies, and low over the grey stone ruins sacked by Morgan, and the hump-backed Puente del Rey, over which the treasure was taken to Portobelo. A giant airliner roared away past us, streaming to another world. Suddenly the tiny, starving peasants' plots ended, and the suburbs began—double concrete garages and gardens set with turquoise swimming-pools.

*　　　*　　　*

'When the Panamanians can cope with collecting their own garbage properly,' said the Major-General, Governor of the Canal Zone and President of the Panama Canal Company, 'they will be fit to run the canal.' A huge Stars and Stripes hung behind his desk, and orange-nosed military aircraft flew past the window, to land on the Canal Zone aerodrome. Over the trees and the roofs of the Zone buildings I could see the funnels of ships moving up to the Miraflores Locks, the first step on their trans-continental journey from the Pacific to the Atlantic.

The relevant garbage was that of a district in Colón, at the other end of the canal, which used to be inhabited and administered by Americans, but which a few years ago was handed over to the Panama government; since then, the streets have become steadily dirtier and the garbage bins are apt to stand by the roadside for days, festering in the tropical heat. The old hospital is empty and its windows broken, and only the Washington Hotel is still just alive, a sad but still noble relic, like a proud old dowager, withered and almost dead; its painted plaster ceilings and tiled walls are cracked, its bar full only of echoes, its lavatories unflushed, and out on the empty terrace the sterile palm trees rattle like old bones; but across the brown water of the Caribbean the big ships steam up to the entrance of the canal, bringing profit to the shareholders of the Panama Canal Company and pride to the Governor. Meanwhile, the garbage goes on festering, and proving that the Panamanians are still far from being competent to run their own canal.

'It takes five years to train my pilots,' said the Governor, 'but the Panamanians change all their civil service whenever they change their President. How do you think I could run the canal if the whole staff was fired every other year?' In Panama the Presidential oath has been administered forty-six times in sixty years.

Only a few Panamanians go to the other extreme from the Governor. One of them, Thelma King, a deputy in the National Assembly, maintains that anything the Egyptians can do, the Panamanians can do too. Nasser is her hero, with Castro a good second, and she often goes across to Cuba for refreshment and relaxation.

Most Panamanians, however, have milder views. All they want is more money without any more responsibility, and a boost to their very uninflated national pride. Their grievances, according to the Governor, are fourfold.

First is the question of sovereignty over the Canal Zone. The burdens of construction, maintenance, operation, sanitation and protection have all fallen on the United States, but why, the
140

Panamanians ask, should it also have sovereignty? The Panama flag, they feel, should fly on all public buildings, and on ships passing through the canal, and Panamanian courts should operate in the Zone for all matters not directly concerned with the administration of the canal.

Secondly, although the annuity has been raised twice from the original quarter of a million dollars to the present figure of just under two million dollars, it is quite unrealistic compared with the same sums that the United States shells out for facilities in other parts of the world—and they quote the eight million dollars rent which they have heard is paid every year for a paltry airfield in Libya. Toll rates have remained the same since the canal was opened in 1914, but with a vast increase in both the number of ships and their individual tonnage the Company's takings have mounted steadily. Panamanians feel that, with their country's geographical position its most valuable asset—in fact the *raison d'être* of the Republic, which until 1903 was merely a province of Colombia—they should get a bigger cut of the profits. Panama means the Canal even more than Honduras means bananas.

Thirdly, there is general discontent about the fact that the average wage for the eight thousand Panamanians working in the Canal Zone is only about a quarter of the average for the three thousand American citizens. And fourthly is the galling clause in the original agreement of 1903 by which the United States was granted the canal concession in perpetuity.

The Governor's reply to these grievances was simply that the United States was within the law, which allowed her the concession of the Canal Zone 'to the entire exclusion of the exercise by the Republic of Panama of any such sovereign rights, power or authority.' 'A law is a law,' he said, adding with a half-smile, half-sigh, that if only everybody agreed with him there would never be any need of lawyers. And anyway, as a gesture, the Panamanian flag had recently been hoisted at one place in the Zone, and was merrily flying there alongside the Stars and Stripes.

The answer to the profits question was that Panama makes a good deal more out of the canal than the two million dollars of the

141

annuity; indirect income—from salaries of Panamanians working in the Zone, purchases of supplies in Panamanian markets, awards of contracts to Panamanian firms and private spending in Panama by American residents of the Zone—amounted to about sixty-five million dollars, which was just about equivalent to the whole of Panama's budget, a fact that Panamanian politicians never seem to remember. Besides, so far from making a fortune out of the canal, the Company only just breaks even. How about putting up the tolls?—to which the Governor, with the same half-smile, replied, 'It would never get through Congress.' Freight rates may have risen since 1914, but the shipping lobby at Washington would see to it that the Panama tolls don't go up too.

As to salaries, American employees mostly fill much higher posts than Panamanians, so a comparison of average wages is unrealistic. Americans and Panamanians are paid the same salary for the same job, with the former getting a twenty-five per cent expatriate allowance and the latter excluded from 'security' jobs. Panamanians are paid much better in the Canal Zone than elsewhere in the Republic, and jobs in the Zone are in great demand. Ordinary labourers, skilled artisans and professional men are all paid more in the Zone than in any other country in Latin America.

As to the perpetuity clause, once again, 'A law is a law.'

But laws have sometimes been changed and treaties have even been cancelled. The small concessions that the United States has granted in the last few years—such as the single Panamanian flag flying in the Zone—have usually come only just in time to avert open antagonism, and with promises of a new American attitude towards Latin America Panamanians feel that now, while tempers are still cool, would be a good time for Washington to offer a fresh treaty. The 1903 treaty was practically Panama's birth certificate, signed when she was hardly experienced in such things, but at a time, as the Panamanian delegate to the United Nations has said, 'marked by ideas, tendencies and procedures, most of which are happily proscribed nowadays in the code of conduct between nations'.

Underneath the ripples blown up by these genuine and understandable feelings is a ground swell driven by the hitherto almost inarticulate force of Panamanian nationalism. In its sixty years of existence, the Republic has been transfixed by a strip of land ten miles wide, owned and ruled by a foreign country. So paramount has that strip been, that the rest of Panama, still almost unchanged since the day Balboa first looked out across the mud and mangroves and saw the Pacific Ocean, has scarcely thought of itself as a country in its own right. There has been no national spirit because there has been no national identity. But things are now moving fast.

More so than the other republics of Central America, Panama has affinities with pre-Castro Cuba. The people of both countries have lived next door to the people of the United States, and the experience, for the poorer neighbour, has been hard to suffer. From their squalor and poverty the Panamanians have looked across the fence and seen a way of life which they had no hope of ever reaching. In Cuba it was the tourist hotels and casinos and night clubs that rankled, and the vision of infinite wealth just beyond the horizon; in Panama it is the suburban complacence of the residential areas of the Canal Zone, the concrete roads and trim lawns, the shrubberies and expensive clubs.

In both cases the comparison was aggravated by a dim suspicion that somehow the poverty of one society was the direct reason for the riches of the other, and that the United States, which derived huge advantage from the arrangement, was not likely to want to upset it. In both cases the country's economy was centred upon one single item, in which the United States was exclusively involved. And in both cases the national rulers—in Cuba a dictator and in Panama a succession of Presidents who changed almost with the frequency of the moon—had brought little relief to their people, found wealth for themselves and appeared to have more than just the connivance of Washington.

To a traveller lately in Cuba, Panama would seem to offer a splendid chance for the United States to display a little of the vision and imagination that might, in the Caribbean not long ago, have prevented disaster and retreat. While the Fidelistas are working away in silence, like white ants in the woodwork, less fanatical men

143

in Panama would welcome the sort of brave gesture that would both foil the extremists and shore up their own tottering faith in the United States; and for the United States it would be a great deal less expensive than obstinacy.

Panamanians are sensitive people, and it is significant that the first issue which brought them clamouring and shouting into the Canal Zone was the question of their flag. Just as a peevish teenager, indignant at being still treated as a baby, turns to sulking, Panama feels that the United States, without going so far as to give her the key of the door, should at least acknowledge some of the facts of adolescence; and on the treatment she gets depends the kind of girl she grows up into. The matter of the Governor's garbage bins is not just an indication of the Panamanians' inefficiency; it is also a symptom of their emotions.

*   *   *

Coffee and doughnuts are served on the railway that runs from Balboa to Colón, alongside the canal; through the maintenance yards, the military camps and aerodromes, the transport depots, the ordnance and engineering shops—cranes, dredgers, tugs, buoys, beacons. Huge tankers slide through the forest beside the train; freighters among the hills; a liner through the trees. In Gatún Lake the stumps of the flooded jungle still poke above the surface; cormorants perch on the treetops, their wings crucified in the sunshine. On every station platform is a little rack with Christian Science literature and tracts.

A bomb on one of the dams, or the wrecking of the locks, would empty the lake, and it would take three years to fill again. Perhaps that is why Russian ships using the canal are subjected to special indignities. An armed guard is put on the bridge with a field radio, and another guard stationed in the engine-room. The pilot's orders are repeated over the radio, just in case the engineer should be tempted to go full speed ahead and ram the lock gates. All cameras are impounded.

' Who were the Allies in the war, and who was defeated? ' cried

144

an indignant Russian captain to his American sentries on passing a German ship, whose crew were all clicking away at him with their Leicas. Whether the object is security, or merely retaliation for similar precautions imposed on American ships in Russian ports, the result is humiliating enough for a ship's captain.

Engineers say that with the exception of some of the electrical gear in the locks there is nothing they would improve on, if they were to rebuild the canal today. It was opened in 1914, and the builders could scarcely have foreseen the tonnage it would have to carry. It is the most spectacular skirmish I have ever seen in the battle of men against geography. The men won, and one of them— a nice detail—was Paul Gauguin; on his way to Tahiti in the 1880s, before the French pioneers were defeated by bankruptcy and yellow fever, he got a job as a navvy digging the cut through the hills.

One thinks of Gauguin again at the sight of the negro girls in the streets of Colon—their silken arms and ear-rings, their rich full bottoms and their rich full negro laughter. They run away, of course, but it seems not so much from modesty or fear as from the timidness of a wild antelope. They are untamed, and yet they are an altogether gentler, prouder animal than the American women in the same streets, with their aluminium voices and their vaccination marks.

There used to be a nationality bar in the Canal Zone—American citizen and non-American citizen—which in fact was almost a colour bar, because the Americans were all white and most of the non-Americans had varying quantities of coloured blood. But when the American forces were integrated and American negroes, citizens of the United States, were posted increasingly to the Canal Zone, with a free run of all facilities, the situation became more embarrassing than even the inhabitants of a Southern-minded territory could suffer; when the nationality barriers were at last lifted the colour problem had already dissolved.

The train journey through the Canal Zone from the Pacific to the Atlantic begins at Balboa Heights, among the spotless gardens and regimented palms, the immaculate boulevards and spacious houses, each with its big car parked in a garage and its baby screaming from

145

behind the mosquito gauze. If the United States only wanted to show off its spick administration it could hardly do it better, and the higgledy-piggledy of Panama City glares enviously through the boundary fence at such luxury.

The journey ends at the Atlantic, by the tourist shops of Colón, with their saris, Benares brassware and ivory elephants. There is a whiff of copra in the air, with just a hint of sandal-wood. Behind are the saloon bars, lined with old photos of tall-funnelled ships steaming up to the Gatún Locks in the early, faded days; and in the back reaches of the town are the slums, terribly poor, dirty and crowded.

Into those slums, by way of the Panamanian press and radio, is poured an undiluted stream of anti-American invective. At a time when the payroll for Panamanians working in the Canal Zone is constantly rising, when the Canal is being deepened and widened by the United States at colossal expense, and when it is annually bringing greater benefits to the people of Panama, those people are being steadily conditioned for even more infectious propaganda from abroad.

So far there has been little enthusiasm for foreign causes, and a demonstration of university students, in a single lordly display of xenophobia, condemned the governments of the United States, Cuba, Russia, Nicaragua, Paraguay, Haiti and the Dominican Republic. But there is a growing though incoherent dissatisfaction which no amount of pamphlets published by the United States Information Services, no amount of proscriptions on pamphlets published in Cuba, no amount of plans for slum clearance published by a government which hasn't got the money to do it anyway and no amount of self-conscious baseball tournaments between Americans and Panamanians, can appease. Panama is impatient for improvement.

IX

Haiti

THE TAXI-DRIVER FROM PORT AU PRINCE AIRPORT
offered me voodoo, folk-dancing, cock-fighting, gambling, Haitian
women, Dominican women, Spanish women, women on women,
men on men and other, less mentionable delicacies. When I showed
no appetite for any of them, he tried another line—a trip up into
the mountains, five thousand feet above the sea. A hotel was all I
wanted for the moment, and when at last he took me to one I found
a Bible on the bedside table. Haiti has something for everybody.

But Haiti has very little for the Haitians. It is a black republic
full of negroes who have lost their most valuable characteristic—
their pride. Where one would expect to find laughter and ebullience,
one finds only tyranny and oppression. Apart from the attractions
listed by the taxi-driver Haiti has nothing to offer but its example.

In the cathedral, full of dark praying figures, a cherubic black
boy slid up to me: 'You wan' nice girl?' He had learnt that much
English. The beggars outside mumbled, 'M'sieur, m'sieur, bon soir,
donne-moi . . .' and then quickly switched to, 'Hi, Joe!' It was a
shock also, after being told for so long to *Tome Coca-Cola*, to *Buvez
Coca-Cola* instead. One was almost tempted to try.

In the public parks, wandering under the trees, sitting on the
grass, students learn their lines. They talk French to the palm trees.
They are banned from politics, so they learn their lines, get their
baccalaureates, put on their white collars, look in vain for jobs and
live for ever in sadness. It is a sad thing to be a student in Haiti.
The huge figures of Haiti's heroes, quite overpoweringly ugly,
glower from their clumsy horses in hilarious attitudes, and offer no
more comfort than the palm trees.

Down by the waterfront, where the tourists used to come ashore in great numbers, and where they still sometimes come in very small numbers, to gasp for a few bewildered, disgusted hours among the voodoo shops and folk craft bazaars, where pimps tail you till you lose your temper, where Haitians live in hutches of sticks and tin and straw separated by channels of alternate mud and dust, where a Methodist missionary helped bravely by a Haitian doctor and dentist and some European ladies but helped not at all by a jealous government runs a dispensary and clinic—down by the waterfront, marked by an immense concrete croquet-hoop across the road, is the Exposition Park.

The Exposition was held in 1949 to prove the success of a century and a half of Haitian independence, and the buildings were left standing to prove the success of the Exposition. Some of them, their concrete cracked, their foundations sinking, their woodwork warped, their gaudy paintwork faded, are now embassies; one of them, apparently empty, is the Legislative Assembly; others are abandoned. Among them, scattered across the threadbare lawns, is a display of statuary that would be funny if it were not so grotesque. An immense square-limbed girl, stark white and cubic with box-like breasts, kneels in the middle of the road lifting a conch, or a torch, or an ice-cream; bronze girls wrestle with sharks; a gilded maiden grapples with a dragon; Simón Bolívar rides a broken-down horse, its head sagging, its feet dragging across the plinth; a man beats a sheaf of swords into a ploughshare; a lion lies down with a lamb; lanky nymphs round a fountain dandle diminutive babies on their knees, and indiscriminately flap their legs and their breasts, the sun catching here a green nipple and there a green toe; red fish frolic with black fish; huge emerald babies with concrete fish-tails and fins for ears roll on their concrete tummies and gambol with emerald dolphins; a student sits between a pair of perky concrete buttocks learning his lines.

I walked past the Presidential palace, a huge white Tuileries with a forecourt a hundred yards deep. In front of it, soldiers stripped to the waist were doing press-ups and arms drill; some were being made to run round the perimeter railings, while the sergeant shouted at them. I stopped to watch, half pitying, half gloating. A

148

sentry shouted at me, raised his rifle and waved me on with it. Nobody was allowed to linger outside the President's railings, or stare at the President's bodyguard.

*   *   *

The man in the palace is Dr. François Duvalier, once a sanitary inspector and now President of Haiti. When he arrived, after ten months in which Haiti had had seven governments, he was welcomed as a strong man, anti-communist and a guarantee of stability, by the United States, which paid the bills, made up the debts and armed and trained the army. If it had been known just how stable he was going to prove, he might not have been hailed so loudly.

One day towards the end of 1960, when he was half-way through his first term as President, he asked the Legislative Assembly to give him full fiscal powers, so that he could run the country's budget on his own. The Assembly refused, and President Duvalier came down from his palace with his Presidential guard, the only efficient body in the country, sat outside the Assembly building with his guns trained on the recalcitrant legislators, and invited them to think again. By the constitution the Assembly was not allowed to vote on the same motion more than once in a session, but on that occasion they voted twice in one evening, and the second time they produced a different answer.

They also signed their own death warrant; they were never convened again. Six months later Duvalier announced that a new single-chamber Assembly would be elected, instead of the old two-chamber Assembly, and it would contain fifty-eight freely elected members.

Even for a part of the world where the art of rigging elections is practised with skill and love, the Haitian election of 1961 was the work of more than just a master. There was no campaign, no parties and no programme. Ballot forms were printed, with the name of Dr. François Duvalier at the top in big letters and the name of one of the fifty-eight candidates below it, in small letters. Nobody was quite certain what that signified, but it was presumed that the candidate was a supporter of Duvalier—not an unlikely possibility.

Election day was announced for a Sunday. Many people, especially among the middle class in Port au Prince, were not expected to vote at all, but a tremendous effort was made to get as many people to the polls as possible. The civil service was told that, though it was Sunday, they would have to go to work, and work meant voting; in many cases they found themselves working on Sunday morning and again on Sunday afternoon. Peasants all over the country were herded to the booths, and as most of them couldn't read anyway, it was not difficult to persuade them, having made their mark, to make it once more for luck, and perhaps a third time too. And even foreigners and tourists—Americans, Canadians, Frenchmen and Italians—were rounded up and pushed along to vote; the alternative to obeying was far worse.

The result of the election, of course, might have been predicted by anyone who knew what they were voting for : a new fifty-eight man Assembly composed of Duvalier's fifty-eight candidates. But the result, in fact, surprised the most cynical electors : Duvalier announced, with gratitude and almost humility, that although he still had another two years in office, the people of Haiti, inspired by God, had decided unanimously to elect him President for a fresh term of six years. The President's emotion was nothing to the electorate's astonishment.

Inauguration day was made an even more sumptuous occasion than election day. Nobody was allowed to leave Port au Prince, and lorry-loads of peasants were brought in from the countryside, to swell the crowds in the streets and possibly to distract attention from the apathetic middle class; most of them had never been to the capital before, and they could be relied on to produce the proper spirit of jubilation. For having expelled the French archbishop and a Haitian bishop Duvalier had recently been excommunicated, but that didn't prevent him calling a *Te Deum* to be sung in the cathedral to celebrate his election, and it did not prevent the Papal Nuncio from attending—under threat of having all the catholic schools in Haiti closed down. And the President, dressed in tails and

150

a top hat, with all his medals on his breast, made a long speech in French, repeating his gratitude and his loyalty, and elaborating the destiny of the Republic.

'United in thought with Me, you have realized, My brother Haitians, the urgency, the necessity of having a Chief chosen by the people, a Chief in whom the majority of the nation, in spite of the quarrels of parties and factions, can recognize the Manager of its essential interests and the dependable Trustee of its destinies . . .

'The people, the army, and you, have chosen Me . . .

'I am facing history; I am facing the nation with a proud head, with a serene soul, a clear conscience and a firm cause . . .

'My brother Haitians! With Me you must procreate, give birth to the new Haiti, and make her live all the great dreams of which she has for too long been frustrated . . .'

None of the peasants, whose only language is creole, could understand a word.

* * *

The army, the traditional guarantor of stability in such countries, has been effectively castrated. In the basement of the Presidential palace is quartered the Presidential guard, about four hundred strong, equipped with the only modern weapons and almost all the ammunition in the country. To call them crack troops would be misleading, but they are as efficient as any soldiers Haiti has ever produced. In the palace stables is a squadron of light tanks.

In addition to the Presidential guard, Duvalier has a court of obsequious attendants who, in order to keep their jobs and make as much money as they can from such funds as are going—taxes, American aid, extortion, bribery—do their paltry utmost to keep him in power. They need him badly, and therefore they praise him. But he has no need of them, for he has something far more effective to ensure his power.

Duvalier's real strength is the huge body of thugs, hoodlums, bogeymen—the *tontons macoutes*. In other dictatorships at least there are institutions—the Church, the universities, a middle class

151

—which maintain some kind of antidote, and possibly even laws, oppressive though they may be. But in Haiti all rule of law is broken, and the population is ruled arbitrarily by an ex-sanitary inspector, with the brutal assistance of his gang of *tontons macoutes*.

People talk of their friends, or their brothers, or their husbands, who disappeared six months ago, even two years ago. 'We hear he is still alive'—but there is no certainty, except the certainty that there was never a trial, and that his life, if it continues, is suffered at the cost of terrible brutality. Information sometimes comes from a prison guard who saw him alive three months ago, but it is better not to hope, and it is better also not to talk; not even to regret, or to mourn, but just pretend that nothing has happened.

'Don't say I told you this,' they say, and look anxiously round the room. 'Say you met my brother in Costa Rica and he told you; don't say anything about me.'

People are hiding in embassies, or are hiding nobody knows where, or have fled to the United States, or have been seen in a village up in the north, or have been beaten to death, or are rumoured to be in Venezuela, or have been heard of in prison, or have been heard of in Mexico, or haven't been heard of at all. Young men who went abroad years ago as students have stayed away. There is no life for them in Haiti; the country has withered under the *tontons macoutes*, President Duvalier's bogeymen, and its people—the cousins of the buoyant, irrepressible, ebullient people of Jamaica, of Trinidad, of the Southern States—have withered too.

An old scholar-diplomat who had written books, attended international conferences and given evidence before the League of Nations, said he had never seen such a plight. He wept for the people of Haiti, 'not because they are my countrymen, not because they are my friends, not because they are black—but because they are men.' By his age and reputation he felt safe to talk, but a mulatto businessman in a Mercedes Benz who had lived for years in London and had been a diplomat in a previous administration, was not so brave. Day after day he promised to tell me about Haiti, and day after day he put it off. Tomorrow we would go up into the mountains in the Mercedes Benz, he said, and there we would be able to talk in peace; but he never came to pick me up, and next time I saw him he said sadly that he had been too busy. Tomorrow—but here it was not safe to talk; the next day—but now it was too hot to talk, and as if to prove it he began to sweat. Then, to appease me, he began to sing gently, 'Cockles and mussels, alive alive-o ! ' and took me to the tennis club.

Then men on the tennis court, and sitting on the club veranda with glasses of whisky and soda, might have been French. They exported coffee and sisal and essential oils, imported British cars, travelled to Europe and sent their children to school in America. They talked disparagingly about the *noirs*, and most disparagingly of all about the *noir* who mattered most. He had a complex, they said, about being a *noir*; even as a sanitary inspector he had never been accepted by the mulatto aristocracy or by the foreigners, or even by the more intelligent *noirs*. Now he was avenging himself of a life of humiliation and ostracism.

But a little gentle criticism, based on colour prejudice, was as far as these prosperous tennis-players were prepared to go. It was frightening to learn that in the long student strike before Duvalier called his 1961 election, when his rule suffered its only real challenge and he had to purge the country not only of an archbishop and a bishop but also of many university professors, intellectuals, priests and some of the best officers in the army, the businessmen of Haiti did nothing.

'Everyone who is not in the government is against it,' said one businessman, but before I had time to ask him how he had shown his hostility at the election he was back on the tennis court.

'In President Magloire's time,' said another, 'we had corruption —just ordinary corruption, like everywhere else. At least the people were reasonably free, even if the government didn't do much to help them, but just stacked up its own fortune. Magloire is in New York now, with nine million dollars in the bank. But under Duvalier it's quite different.'

'Have you heard about Cromwell James? ' asked a third. 'He was a British subject, from Granada, and he was taken one night

153

by the *tontons macoutes* and beaten up in the Presidential palace. He died of gangrene. Gangrene of the buttocks. Oh yes, the British ambassador has protested—no trial, no conviction, no habeas corpus, and all that sort of thing. But what's the use? '

'We have a superficial veneer of French culture,' said a particularly sententious man, ' pasted over an instinctive African culture, and the mixture is trying to reconcile itself to a political alignment with the Organization of American States. It's hopeless, quite hopeless.'

'What we really need is foreign investment,' said a man who owned a factory, and then, to draw attention from the fact that he was busily investing all his own money in the United States, he said that the trouble with Duvalier was that nobody had really given him a chance. If only the opposition would let up for a while, so that the President could spend more time governing the country and less time fighting his enemies, then Haiti might regain a little prosperity.

It seemed superfluous to remind such a man that Duvalier had already had four years, and that opposition could scarcely be described as active. A middle class revolution in Haiti is as unthinkable as a palace revolution or a military *coup d'état*, let alone a peasants' revolt. The bourgeoisie is as cowed as the proletariat, and though they all know that things are getting worse, and that there is no hope of things ever getting better, they are too terrified to move. It is safer to stick to tennis.

With more whisky some of them became a little bolder, but though they had nothing but hatred and contempt for President Duvalier it was obvious that he never need mistake the grievances of the mulatto businessmen for a threat.

'He's not even like Trujillo, in the Dominican Republic, who has at least brought efficiency to his country. But here nothing works—the electricity has broken down, the telephone is in a mess . . .'

'And America's in his hands. If they stopped giving him his pocket money he'd just snap his fingers and call in the other side. Russia would love to pay, or China. He's not above blackmail, and the priests are already saying that he's a communist. You never know.'

Suddenly it began to rain, and the tennis-players ran for shelter. The deluge dropped in a solid mass of water, beating on the trees, splashing in the sudden brown puddles and blowing like a mist sideways under the club veranda. Even indoors it was wet and cool during the storm. As suddenly the rain stopped, and there was the sun again, shining on the glistening leaves, and the humming-birds back at the bougainvillaea. The world was cleaner, washed of its dust and dripping with pleasure, satisfied and panting a little from exhaustion. Rich smells drifted across the tennis courts, and it was hot again, but with a new fresh heat, ready to begin again. And for half an hour the storm hung across the end of the sky, like a sin.

It would be nice to think of Dr. François Duvalier and his *tontons macoutes* passing like a sudden, dreadful storm.

*   *   *

There were two characteristics of Port au Prince that I liked. One was the old architecture, especially of the pretty houses standing round the park. They are shamelessly French, tall with wooden balconies and high, steep gables, sometimes slanting into even steeper gables, decorated with marvellous, impossibly intricate fret-work eaves. The bigger houses stand in symmetrical gardens, like a page out of a child's story-book, and almost as flimsy. One expects to see an old woman in a wimple walk up the path, or a blonde princess come to the balcony and throw down a letter. It is im-possible, looking at one of those houses, to think of the *tontons macoutes*.

The other was the habit of Haitians to indulge in swank. ' We are the second oldest republic in America, after the United States,' they boast, but that is not nearly good enough for most of them : ' We had free education in Haiti before you had it in England.' But the biggest claim is still more startling : ' Even the British Commonwealth is a Haitian idea. Toussaint L'Ouverture proposed the idea of a commonwealth to France, but it was rejected, and then

155

England took it up a hundred and fifty years later. And now look at France! In the African colonies she too has adopted Toussaint's advice. He was a great man, but he was years before his time. The world has only just caught up with him.'

Happily, in most respects the world has far to go, to catch up with Haiti.

*   *   *

After his excommunication President Duvalier sent his children to the Methodist mission school, and ordered armed guards to patrol outside the school gates. I went one morning to the six-o'clock service in the Methodist church, full of people singing, 'Once in Royal David's City' in creole with almost unstifled happiness, offering spontaneous prayers, joining in the responses, and wandering gaily in and out of the church. For the first time I saw a hint of the latent African joy that I had hoped still smouldered beneath all the smothering misery. Perhaps Duvalier's children had noticed it too.

The Methodist minister, after nearly thirty years in Haiti, was appalled at the terror which had struck the country, and told me almost unbelievable stories of persecution. But his experience and love of Haiti did not let him be distracted from the deeper, older problems. First was that of language; ninety per cent of the population was illiterate and spoke only creole, but there was no official acknowledgement of the existence of creole, and all government proclamations, all Duvalier's speeches, all education and all newspapers were in French. Second was the density of the population—more people than in the Dominican Republic next door, but living in a smaller area. Third was the archaic methods of agriculture and the fragmentation of the land; ploughing was often done with machetes, crop rotation was unknown, the forests were being rapidly destroyed, and despite attempts by the American aid mission to diversify the economy by planting more sisal and cocoa there had so far been little enthusiasm from either the Haitian government or the peasants.

The official at the American aid headquarters was a negro; he was in an anomalous position—a black man administering a white country's aid to a black state. But three years of doing it had brought only disillusionment; the corruption of Haitian politicians and the absence of all morality had saddened a good, despairing man. That the fortunes made by unscrupulous Haitian officials were not bigger was simply because Haiti was such a poor country. In the eighteenth century it had been the pride of the French empire, the richest colony in the western hemisphere, but after the Haitian negroes turned against their French masters and slaughtered them, they pulled the wool over the world's eyes; and they were pulling it still. Haiti was now exporting only two-thirds of the quantity of coffee she had exported in the eighteenth century, and sugar production too was less than in colonial times. For a hundred and fifty years the country had rotted.

But he blamed the United States almost as much as Haiti; America had had no right to sit there all those years, growing fat and sending nothing but tourists to goggle at the voodoo exhibitions. Recently money had been poured in, but it had gone down the drain of corruption; he was sickened by three years of sitting at meetings with Haitian government officials, knowing that they were lying to him, and knowing that they knew that he knew they were lying. Signs of a change in Washington since the Kennedy administration had brought not the flicker of a change in Haiti.

'They still have a "slave unbound" complex,' he said. 'If you remonstrate with them, or criticize them, they answer, "You only say that because I'm black". The whole country is built on that sort of feeling.'

He was a black man who said it.

*   *   *

Cap Haitien, on the north coast of Haiti, might still be a French colonial port, with its golden eighteenth century streets and its balmy waterfront. But the opera house where Orfée once wept for Eurydice has been closed for more than a century and a half, and the antics first of a depraved society of white men and then of the intoxicated society of black men who dispossessed them, are long forgotten. There only remain the stunned, mute unhappiness of the inheritors, and the ruins. An American destroyer lay at anchor in the harbour and half the crew was ashore, drunk.

A few miles inland, at the foot of a mountain, is the carcase of a palace, with baroque steps, balustraded terraces and the remnants of grandeur. It is called Sans Souci, with just presumption, and was the work of King Henri Christophe. A few years ago, to celebrate a hundred and fifty years of freedom, it was lit up with coloured lights and flood-lamps, and Marian Anderson sang *Ave Maria* to fifty thousand ecstatic people.

At six in the morning I left the palace and walked up the mountain to the Citadel. It was like walking through Africa—through coffee and banana gardens, with black families living in huts in the forest and chickens scuttling in the undergrowth.

Two hours later, drenched with sweat, I reached the fortress. Henri Christophe, who had been a slave of the French, built it with the labour of his countrymen, who now served a king, to defend himself against Napoleon, who never came. It is gigantic, like a vast stone battleship stranded on a peak, its prow high in the Caribbean sky and its cannons ranged in huge galleries and pointing down into the jungle. Massive pyramids of cannon balls lie untouched, slightly rusting. The mist swirled over the ramparts, round the towers and battlements, across the empty courtyards, and water dripped petulantly in the dungeons. There was a sudden flash of sunlight through a gateway, but the bang never came. I had the Citadel to myself.

Duvalier—if only he had built a Citadel, and died! Walking down the forest path I met an American sailor in white uniform riding up on a pony. Behind him, trotting barefoot in the heat, followed a Haitian negro, with a bucket of iced Coca-Cola on his head. The sailor stopped to talk.

He was from the destroyer in the harbour, and was in a hurry. His ship was due to sail at noon. Where to? He guessed he didn't know, maybe just a patrol along the coast, to the Dominican Republic or

158

some place. There was going to be trouble, that was for sure. What sort of trouble? Hadn't I heard the news? Why, that guy Trujillo had been assassinated. Dictator for more than thirty years, and they'd got him at last. It comes to all of them in the end. The sailor kicked his pony on up the path, and I bought a Coca-Cola from the negro. It was the first I had ever had.

X

Dominican Republic

EL BENEFACTOR—THE MAN WHO RULED THREE million of his countrymen for thirty-one years, the generalissimo who gave his name to their capital and to everything else in the land from an aerodrome to an era, whose effigy stood in every public place and whose portrait hung in every private parlour, who with his family controlled all the country's industry and owned a third of the cultivable land, who had exiled or imprisoned or executed his enemies, who was believed to have made nearly three hundred million pounds out of it, who was the adulated, venerated, execrated, hailed and hated epitome of a nation, the Father of the Fatherland —El Benefactor had been dead six days.

For six days the people of the Dominican Republic had been deprived of the one constant in their lives. Longer than the subjects of either Mussolini or Franco, almost three times longer than those of Hitler, they had been ruled by a dictator so omnipotent that a life without him was a life quite uncontemplated. Only the oldest generation could remember what it had been like before Trujillo came; for the rest there had been no hope of his ever going, simply because there had been no thought of ever hoping. The old had lost all habit of freedom, the middle-aged and young had never learnt it. The future had been in his hands; the years were measured by his reign.

Now, suddenly, his death had given them back a future—raw and strange and profoundly baffling. The predicament was bewildering, the implications mystifying, the responsibility frightening. To rejoice was as unthinkable as it was impossible. The Dominicans were stunned.

Probably the only people who had joined in the universal adoration with sincerity were his family, the oligarchy of sycophants and profiteers and the officers of the army. But with tyranny Trujillo had brought stability, and the middle class, though intellectually and politically frustrated, had little to complain of. For the mass of the people, the peasants and workers, he was a demi-god, hypnotic and pervasive.

His crimes were those of all dictators—murder, imprisonment, banishment, the ruthless extinction of all opposition and the relentless appropriation of the country's riches. But ironically his biggest crime was that for a long time he was a success. By doing well for himself he did well, materially, for the country too. The machine, infernal though it may have been, worked efficiently and the Dominican Republic, richer than most of its neighbours, prospered. Of course, during those same thirty years most other countries in the world also advanced, but the progress of the Dominican Republic from chaos and economic poverty to a prosperity that could not fail to benefit even the peasants, was all the work of El Benefactor. Brutal autocracy brought material development, and that development, in the distorted context of Latin American politics, could be seen to justify the brutality. The criminal became a precedent for progress.

Towards the end of his reign, because of an even bigger budget for the army and police after two invasions of the country had been attempted from Cuba, and because of the growing caution of foreign investors, the progress ceased. But admirers of Trujillo—and they were sometimes the most improbable people—could still point with glee to the assets.

'Look,' they cried, 'the streets are clean!' Yes, even six days after the era ended, the streets were clean. And the officials were courteous and efficient, the electric light went on, the two-way concrete highway had no pot-holes, there was nobody sleeping on the pavements, and when you pulled the plug the cistern flushed. Confronted by such happy facts, even after allowances for the shock of coming straight from Haiti, it was hard to remember all the liabilities.

But officially the era was not ended. The drummer had stopped, but the soldiers, each with their black arm-bands, marched on, keeping in step for a while out of habit. ' Trujillo will live for ever in the hearts of all Dominicans ! ' was hung in coloured lights across the army barracks, and one almost believed he would. The newspapers, which day after day managed to reveal still gorier details of the assassination, vied with each other to print the thickest black frames and shed the greatest grief. Photo supplements of El Benefactor's achievements and incidents from his life's service to the country were filled out with column upon column of laments from his bereft subjects and turgid messages of condolence from his admirers—package lots from government offices, shops and business firms, individual telegrams from American soldiers, Hollywood actresses, and General Franco.

The adulation of his lifetime, the honours, titles, decorations, the huge albums of photographs left in every hotel bedroom, the pageants, receptions and all the obsequiousness were equalled only by the even more sickening panegyrics after his death. It seemed doubtful if canonization—even apotheosis—would be enough for El Benefactor, and the biggest wreath was laid in a monumental editorial : ' In the annals of twenty centuries of Christianity two men alone have achieved resurrection—Jesus Christ crucified on Calvary, and now Trujillo, sacrificed on the tragic night of May 30th, 1961. And just as that son of Joseph, in two thousand years, was followed by no other Christ, so too there will be none to follow the Christ of the Dominicans, who gave himself in goodness, love, piety, mercy and justice; because, like Jesus, Trujillo was good and just.'

By Christmas of that year the capital of the Dominican Republic was called no longer Ciudad Trujillo, but Santo Domingo, its name for four hundred years, and the body of Rafael Leonidas Trujillo had been taken by his lonely, sorrowing family and buried in Paris.

*　　　*　　　*

Whatever the truth of the assassination, it had been a bungled

162

business. Some of the assassins were killed, others captured later; four of them bullied an unhappy doctor, half English, into sheltering them in his house, and after they had fled from him he cut his wrists and throat, because the publicity, or possibly the shame, was too much for him.

Fifty foreign journalists dashed in a cavalcade of taxis from mortuaries to press conferences, from embassies to hospital bed-sides, for inspections of the bullet-riddled car in which Trujillo had been attacked, and of the bullet-riddled bodies of selected assassins. Diplomats cursed the journalists and asked them what they thought, and the journalists cursed the Dominican officials and asked them what they thought, and nobody asked the Dominican people what they thought, or even cursed them.

The local papers said that the assassination was part of an inter-national plot, and the foreign journalists said that they only said that to produce more scapegoats. Trujillo's elder son, Ramfis, said that he had no desire to become dictator in his father's place, and an American said that, if he had inherited as many million dollars as Ramfis and knew as much about the world's night clubs and the world's movie actresses, he wouldn't either. Ramfis, who was in Paris at the time of the assassination, also said that he wanted to serve his country, and he was promptly made commander-in-chief of the armed forces, although as a student at an American military college he had spent most of his time nipping off to Hollywood, and as head of the air force he had never learnt to fly; but the Trujillo family wanted him there, and so did the army, even if it only meant that all the old generals could watch him like a lot of hungry lions.

A German businessman, who had been a Luftwaffe pilot and after the war found Trujillo's country a congenial place to settle in, said that the Dominican Republic's most desperate need was for under-standing, good will and generous, intelligent aid from the United States. A Belgian businessman said, in a whisper, that I should be careful who I talked to, and what I said. The President of the Republic said that nobody should hesitate to denounce any abuse of privilege by government officials, or be afraid to complain of any hardship. A diplomat said that the President was an intellectual, incorruptible, patriotic and weak, and that, together with the general willingness among the government and even among the army officers to avoid a revolution, he was the biggest hope for a peaceful advance to democracy. A Dominican said that I had simply no idea of the strength of the family bond in Latin America, and that the Trujillos were united by something far more powerful than personal gain or jealousy. A Bolivian journalist who lived in Venezuela and worked for a Brazilian paper said that he had been shown plenty of bodies but none of them had been Trujillo's, which proved that he had died of a heart attack and that the assassination story had been put out by the Trujillo family to give them an excuse for getting rid of all their enemies. All the cinemas were closed, and the radio played incessant Beethoven symphonies, with occasional lapses into Bach.

An American journalist said in a cable to his paper that Trujillo's younger son had gone off his head at the news of his father's death, had seized a machine-gun and shot down thirty convicts in the local prison before being put in a padded cell. A Dominican official said there was no end to the irresponsibility of American journalists, that nothing had changed in the Dominican Republic but that everything was now different, that they were anxious to impress the world of the country's stability and good faith, that the Organization of American States was welcome to send a delegation to inspect the country, and that the United States could even send an ambassador again. A French journalist said that the late dictator's younger brother could summon up an army of machete-swinging peasants at any time he liked, and that it was a terrible pity that the local papers couldn't spray a little real blood on to every copy. A Dominican official said that there was no end to the irresponsibility of French journalists either.

An American paper said that fighting had broken out in part of the Dominican Republic, and the Dominican ambassador to Persia, who was not at his post, said that it was nonsense, that the whole country was under control, and that he would provide free transport to anywhere any American journalist liked and show him the truth. The head of the secret police, who controlled a radio station and a newspaper and who was once the second most powerful and perhaps the first most hated man in the land, was dismissed and sent to a post in the Dominican embassy in Tokyo; and an Englishman who knew about these things said he would never reach Japan, but would end up in Belgium, where he had a friend who controlled an international gang of racketeers.

*   *   *

Those journalists and television men horrified me. They all lived together in a big empty hotel, whose only other guest was a sad-eyed American spinster. They hung around in the foyer for announcements of press conferences, swinging their cameras and transistor radios, whispering at the bar, waiting for long-distance calls, jumping whenever a page-boy came through with his black-board and bicycle bell, exchanging rumours and theories and tele-phone numbers in undertones, abusing the English language and being discourteous, crude and thoughtless. Human beings meant nothing to them. Their values were only news values, dwindling with the minutes and expressed in terms of the 'story' they were on. For them a story was a taxi ride, a cruel inquisition of a man half dead in a prison cell, a twisted, uncouth cable. They were un-interested in issues, reactions, effects; they had no time to think, and no feelings for other people's feelings. Details, clues, calumnies—they threw all the scraps into a stew-pot of facts, an amorphous mass of knowledge without sense, and from it, at regular hours through the day, they pulled their cables.

The machines in the cable office of the hotel clattered, the exor-bitant taxi-drivers outside waited for chances to cash in on gulli-bility and desperation, a fountain splashed drearily, a little pimp standing just inside the big glass doors offered delights which none of the journalists had time for. In the hotel tourist shop a bored half-caste girl dozed behind her wicker baskets and silly hats, like a bad Gauguin. Round the empty swimming-pool television teams set up their cameras and conducted futile interviews with men who didn't matter, and two German girls walking across the grass, nym-

165

phets with delicious, breathless, bathing-suit bodies, passed un-noticed.

One afternoon all the journalists grabbed their notebooks, cameras and side-kicks, and tore through Ciudad Trujillo in taxis to a military hospital in a big army camp. One of the assassins, a shaven-headed man with bullets in his stomach, was lying sweating with pain and terror in a small white-washed room. A doctor and a nurse were crushed into a corner, astonished, as the journalists swept in over the assassin's bed, their ballpoint pens at work and their microphones crammed to the unhappy man's face. The little room was filled with exploding flashlight bulbs, whirring cameras, men climbing over the hospital furniture to plug their equipment into electrical fittings, shouted orders, shouted translations, shouted questions, and feeble, agonized answers.

' So, you say you were just an accomplice in the plot? Well, who was the chief? The brother? Whose brother? The brother of an individual. What's that, the brother of an individual? Will you translate that for us? The chief was the brother of an individual? An individual in the government? An individual in the army? But what was the point of it all, the object? Why did you kill him? You didn't mean to kill him? Get that, Bud? They didn't mean to kill him. Let's have that one again, I wasn't switched on. The brother of an individual? Hell, no, they didn't mean to kill him. Will you stop that camera, I can't hear a thing. What did you mean to do? Oho, just kidnap him? Mind your head, that fellow, you're in my picture. But why kidnap him? This is the worst interview I've had in years. Oho, I see. But what went wrong? The lights failed? What lights? You never said anything about lights. The signals failed, he says. The signals failed, Bud. Three flashes on the car lights, but they failed. You only meant to kidnap him anyway? Will you translate that for us? The signals failed. But what was the purpose? Oho, I get it. *Libertad*. But *libertad* from what? I know what? No, I don't know what. You tell me. *Libertad* from you know what. That's what he says, Bud, *libertad* from you know what. Let's have it again, for the tape. What's that? Translate for Christ's sake, translate. You guys in front there, you've had enough, clear
166

away and let the rest of us in. Was it an international plot. Were there any foreigners involved in it? No? He says no, Bud. From Venezuela? No? Not from Venezuela either, Bud. *Libertad* from you know what, that's what he said. Just one more picture, with the bandages. Hell, I want the bandages. How many bullets, doctor? You only tried to kidnap him? What the hell's *libertad* anyway? '

Out in the hospital corridor, with the journalists who couldn't squeeze into the room, was a little elderly American, tired and hunted and wearing a black cravat, with a little wife in a black dress. They had been coming to the Dominican Republic for years, since Trujillo first cleared the place up and made it safe for foreigners. They had known him well, he was a close friend of theirs, and he had visited with them in Phoenix, Arizona. He was a great man. Yes, sir, he was a great man. What I'd call a great man. They had had lunch with him last Tuesday, the day he was assassinated. Just seven and a quarter hours later, sir. Yes, he was what I'd call a great man. I've never known anybody like him, sir, no. That's right, I've never known anybody like him.

*   *   *

At Ciudad Trujillo airport passengers coming off planes were led to a table in the immigration office. The man behind the table asked you if you had read that notice, and pointed to a board high on the wall, telling foreigners always to carry their passports with them. As you looked up sideways to read it a hidden camera took a photograph, for the record.

Tyranny was equally invisible outside the cathedral, where Columbus is supposed to be buried. Men sat in twos and threes on the benches, some of them in straw boaters, and in the middle the Discoverer, in a doublet with his hand on a capstan, lunged at the darkening sky. A naked Indian girl, clinging to a ledge of the pedestal, scratched his name with a shaky hand—Cristóbal Colón.

On the ninth day of mourning for El Benefactor a requiem mass was held in the cathedral. An immense crowd came to the square and watched silently as the President and members of the Trujillo

167

family went inside. There was no noise, except the deep cathedral bell and the shuffling of feet. There was no grief either, but just perplexity, and when the mass was over the square was emptied of people and filled instead with a great silence, heavy like an imminent thunderstorm.

I tried to take a photograph of the sixteenth century gateway of a barracks on which was hung a banner, ' Always Trujillo ! ' There were two soldiers lolling outside, and as soon as I raised my camera they raised their rifles. Sergeants appeared at every window in the street, shouting, whistling and waving. I fled into a bar where three young Americans were pouring dimes into a row of fruit machines, kicking and punching and cursing them, pouring more dimes in and ordering more beer. The barman was enjoying it, but the beer was frozen beyond all flavour, and I started to sneeze. ' Always Trujillo ! '—and the egg-shaped head, tapering upwards, of the dead dictator turned a dead stare from the wall above the bar.

' Trujillo, your people adore you ! '

' Trujillo, we are proud to be your sons, now and for ever ! '

The hoardings in the countryside jarred with the primitive wooden huts, the barefoot peasants, the naked children, the ragged old men. With an English journalist who was desperate to get away from the ' story ' and who had heard rumours of a mysterious Foreign Legion camped on a plain among the mountains, I drove up to Constanza, a town in a valley that might have been in Savoy. Every few miles we were stopped by military check posts. Men poked guns and bullock faces through the car windows, and fumbled their triggers with clumsy fingers; we looked down the muzzles and knew, as they knew, that if a bullet went off nothing would happen to them. At each post they made us open the boot of the car. Trujillo's body had been found in the boot of a car.

We stopped for beer at village shops, waved at the girls, made funny little English jokes for each other and stopped for more beer. Through mist and up a steep escarpment we came to another land, where peasants rode donkeys across fields of oats. In the middle stood a monument to El Benefactor—' Always Trujillo ! '—and a Beau Geste fort with soldiers along the battlements pointing guns at us.

We marched in, and up a turret staircase to a little room where we had an absurd conversation with a bucolic lieutenant. Was this the Foreign Legion? No, but there had been one here once, at the time of the invasion from Cuba in 1959. Who were the foreigners? Oh, just foreigners.

In the mist the valley became less like Savoy and more like Scotland. Half a mile away was a white concrete hotel, with a dining-room laid for hundreds and a lavatory like something from a model dairy farm. We had it all to ourselves, and drank rum at the bar and Chianti with our chicken. In the afternoon, as we rolled down the escarpment from the hills there was a glimpse of the sunlit plain through the mist, but now it was like the Thames valley, and we stopped for a sentimental look at it, and to get rid of some of the beer and rum and wine, and when we got back into the car we talked about a girl in England.

At the check posts on the way back we were as rude as we dared to the soldiers who thumbed our passports and opened the boot. In the suburbs of Ciudad Trujillo sentries patrolled round every house belonging to members of the government and of the Trujillo family. 'Always Trujillo!'—and happily we waved a lordly hand.

XI

Puerto Rico

'WHY IS IT THAT NOBODY LIKES US?' ASKED A SAD American editor in San Juan. 'We can't do anything—anything at all—without people jumping at our throats. And just look what the Russians get away with! All we want to do is help. And the best way we know is the dollar. But the word dollar is an infectious disease. It's abominated.'

'You can't treat these Latinos as human beings,' said another American, who in his time had worked for both Batista and Trujillo. 'I know. I know 'em all, from the Magellan Straits to Mexico. Ninety per cent of 'em are sub-human, and the rest are crooks. What they need is somebody to crack the whip. Now take Trujillo. He was a much maligned man.'

'Yes,' said a German, 'dictators are best.'

Puerto Rico, as they keep on telling you, is not a territory; and although at first you are puzzled, you gradually begin to see what they mean. It is a kind of lost love-child, born to the Spanish Empire and fostered by the United States. Its people, who have the second highest per capita income in Latin America and one of whom is American ambassador to Venezuela, are citizens of the United States, but they pay no federal taxes and they have no vote in Washington.

It is the home of Operation Bootstrap, a gigantic development programme that lifted the country out of the mud in twenty years, and of Operation Serenity, 'the programme of spiritual development that goes hand-in-hand with economically-oriented Operation Bootstrap.' It has the finest old Spanish town and the squalidest old American slums I saw on my whole journey, it is the pride and the embarrassment of a colonial power that falls over backwards to admit to none of the classical sentiments of an empire, it is the playground of thousands of tourists who used to go to Cuba, it is the political property of a wily Governor who knows a good thing when he sees one (and the United States is the best thing in sight), it is officially a Commonwealth within the American union, and it produces a quarter of all the brassières worn in the United States. No, Puerto Rico is definitely not a territory.

Down by the San Juan waterfront the mooring warps creek in the Atlantic wind, and well-fed cockroaches waddle across the cobbles, hell-bent for the neon lights of a night club or a brothel. In the dark bars of the old town, half the girl students wear crew cuts and carry books about child psychology; the other half look like Jackie Kennedy. And in the squares, among the trees and pretty houses, the old men stand and watch the public television sets.

*   *   *

I was told that I should go and see La Perla, as if she was a gypsy fortune-teller, or a blue film. I was directed through an arch in the twenty-foot thick walls of the old Spanish city and found her clinging to the cliffs above the Atlantic breakers—a settlement of shacks. The road narrowed to a lane, then to a path, finally to a plank forming a broken cat-walk over the mud and mess. Naked children, oblivious of their tragedy, played in the sun, in the squalor. Half a rusty car lay on its back, as though it had been tipped from the fortress walls above. Old creatures in bare feet stood silently at the entrance of tiny wooden shops, or pecked at empty tins.

I pushed through a group of women standing in the path. One of them, a hag with scabs on her face, shot out a skinny arm, clutched my jacket and begged for money. I was frightened of my riches, and tore myself away. The path got narrower. People watched me in silence. Were they people?

'Can I get through this way?'

'Yes, yes,' they murmured vacantly.

The path got more and more foul, the shacks filthier. It was worse than tragic; it was absurd to see people living in such things. I felt like remonstrating with them, asking them what the hell they thought they were doing there. Why didn't they go and live in a new block of flats? Didn't they know they were American citizens?

I longed to take photographs, but I didn't dare get my camera out. Little black eyes followed me, and silent children stood in the path and watched me go by. The only noise was from the Atlantic breakers. I walked faster, more desperately, trying to find a way through.

Suddenly everything changed. It was I who was obscene, not them; I in my coat and tie and trousers, with my Leica and my suede shoes. I had been terrified, now I was ashamed. To take photographs would be an insult, an affront to any dignity they had left. Who was I to focus their misery and record it, to be tut-tutted over in a London flat? I came to a group of young men. Their look of offence was too much, and I turned back.

It meant passing the hag again. She shot out the skinny arm and seized my hand; I wrenched it away, and she seized my jacket and ripped the pocket. The other women just watched in silence. The only noise was from the Atlantic breakers and the sound of my jacket tearing.

I escaped. Above, in the grey sky over the fortress walls, sailed the Stars and Stripes. I had been with La Perla for just three minutes.

*   *   *

A mile or two along the coast from La Perla is Condado, a ribbon of beaches, rocky coves and concrete hotels. In the darkened bars the noise of the sunlit breakers is taken up by the rattle and hiss of tinny air-conditioning machines. Tourists sit deprived of the smell of seaweed, locked up in their chilly padded boxes and gazing across their Scotch-on-the-rocks, through the sunproof windows to the Atlantic. Or they sit in the hotel lobbies, waiting to fall in at the tour guide's command. The men's Hawaiian shirts are sadly out of tune with their sagging shoulders and hungry faces; women wear Bermuda shorts who might look better in crinolines. There are a few honeymoon couples in identical shirts and shorts, their fingers interlocked; and a blue-rinsed woman clutching a folksy wicker basket, with a husband clutching the *Wall Street Journal*. The silly modernistic lamps and decorations already look old fashioned; and anyway they are falling to bits. In the cafeterias they give you little squares of tasteless butter, served on bits of cardboard. Life is a pale whisper, like the discreet recorded music. Only the massage shops and beauty salons are operating at full pitch. God knows, there's a need.

But down the road, if you are lucky, you suddenly see the sun shining on a silver sea, a Spanish fortress on a rock, a web of breakers rolling on the beach, a sailing-vessel dipping towards the harbour, a grey-haired old negro lying like a dog in a shady doorway, a pirate selling pineapples, a pretty girl walking through the sunshine and all the loafers watching her. And then the concrete hotels dissolve, and with them the flabby tourists, and even one's own confusion with dimes and nickels.

*   *   *

In the cathedral square of Havana, on my last night in Cuba, I had heard Rostropovich playing his cello to the stars, and to the people. In Puerto Rico, at San Juan university, I heard another man, the master of another age, play to a very different audience. Seats cost five dollars and there was a smell of spearmint in the air.

' When we came down from New York to live here, I thought I'd miss the theatres and the music and all that. But boy! Whatta we get? The best! '

' Mary, you really shouldn't have put on petticoats,' said a man behind me.

In the middle of the platform was a cello, with the bald head of Casals above it. He stuck out his lower lip furiously; a rage boiled inside him, perhaps because his fingers wouldn't work as they used to. But he need not have worried; it was part of Operation Serenity, and he played Beethoven, Vivaldi and Haydn. In the interval a great tropical rainstorm fell, and we all stood in the cloisters looking out at it beating in the palms. And afterwards, as I walked across

173

the campus to catch a bus, huge cold raindrops fell out of a starry sky and the cicadas sang with pleasure.

Next night I went again. To retaliate against the spearmint I had had a supper of shrimps and raw onions, but I regretted it. A ravishing girl with immense brown eyes sat down next to me, and almost immediately asked to change seats with her mother, who waved her fan in my face through the whole concert.

But I didn't care. Casals played Handel and Bach, and next day I was going back to Cuba.

XII

Cuba: Havana Again

THE NOTICE AT HAVANA AIRPORT—'DEATH TO THE invader!'—had a new meaning. In the two and a half months that I had been away Cuba had been invaded; and Cuba had smashed the invasion. Many of the invaders had been killed, and twelve hundred of them were in prison. But the most surprising thing, after all the stories I had heard about refugees clamouring to leave, was the number of Cubans on the plane returning to Cuba from Miami. I too, if I were a Cuban, would prefer to live in Cuba.

Altogether—and quite apart from the prejudices that I brought with me from nine other countries—Cuba was a very different place from the country I had left. There was a new reassurance in the air, a self-confidence that was refreshing after the former uncertainty and bewilderment, and doubly so after the apathy and amorality of the other countries. The people of Cuba had survived the invasion which they knew was coming, and at last they knew where they stood, and who stood with them. There was now no alternative to the revolution, and being Cuban they were going to enjoy it. *Como no?* Who cared if the cars did break down, or even the economy, if the economy only meant a new car? Anyway, Russia would keep them going; they had half the world on their side.

In the shop windows there were notices in Russian, and a Soviet Cinerama programme was being advertised; a Czech exhibition was being held in the Palacio de Bellas Artes, where the Chinese exhibition had been before. The bar where one had been able to buy *Time* magazine now sold only Russian and Chinese papers.

'Try our Gagarin cocktail!'

'Fly to Prague!'

'I love you,' said a fair young man, tapping me on the arm in the bar of the Habana Libre hotel. He wore a loose Hawaiian shirt, and was with a pretty girl in tight black slacks; they were very sun-burnt, and carried bathing towels in a basket. 'I love you,' and before I could recover he added, 'I love you Rudyard Kipling, I love you Lucky Jim.'

I shook his hand, and he said, 'Yevgeny Yevtushenko. I am Russian poet. I love you John Osborne, you John Wain, you beat-niks. I love people. People are good.' Then he leaned over the bar, held up two fingers and said, 'Tom . . . Collins . . . Two!'

There were more people in the bars and restaurants; not just the dice-rollers helping themselves to the bottles of Scotch in front of them, but customers who brought more scope for the barman's art—a glass of rum and ice, a spoonful of cream, a few cherries, a dash of liqueur, a squeeze of juice and a twist of a leaf. And at night the whole city seemed to be chattering under the trees in the Prado. A block of flats with a broken neon sign and no lights in the windows stood empty; the owners were in Miami, and Cuba was glad they had gone.

'I think you are English,' said a happy man who came up to me in the street. 'No? Well then, Canadiense? Holland? Russki? Polski? Czecho? No? Well then, you know one thing? You look like an Englishman.'

'It's just the season,' said a British diplomat. 'It's the summer.'

If the people who had been for the revolution were now reassured, those against it were finally silenced. It was nice not to be pestered by counter-revolutionaries and disgruntled capitalists with a moan. In a gigantic swoop during the invasion a hundred thousand of them had been rounded up and imprisoned for a week or two in the moat of the Morro fort, and the experience had had its effect. Their last demonstration was marked by a huge hole in the middle of Havana's main shopping centre where El Encanto, the biggest department store in the town, had once stood; it had taken only two hours to burn out. Cubans who couldn't do without it were lining up with the weeping women outside the Ministry of Foreign Affairs for passports, or waiting at dawn outside the airline offices for tickets to Miami. But all planes were booked up for the next eight months. The revolution had won.

I went to see the beautiful Spanish girl in the Casa de las Americas. 'There are no bombs in the night now,' she said, flashing those mesmerizing eyes. During the invasion she had carried on working in her office until one day, from her flat at the top of a skyscraper, she saw three American warships out at sea. That riled her. 'I was crazy, just crazy.' She put on *miliciana* uniform, went off to the invasion front and dressed the soldiers' wounds. Now she was pleased with herself, and with her country. Like other Cubans who had been apprehensive about the invasion and uncertain how they would themselves behave when it came, she was now reassured. The revolution was safe, and the invasion had sealed it.

'When socialism goes along with patriotism, it works,' said an English socialist. 'Look at Russia, China—and now Cuba.'

'I should like to have both Rostropovich and Casals playing in Havana,' said another English socialist.

* * *

I remembered Gloria, and went to her little night club, but though there were still half a dozen disconsolate girls she wasn't among them, and I was the only customer. No one knew what had happened to Gloria. I sat down at the bar and was given a drink in a glass advertising a brand of shampoo, with instructions painted on it. A rather worn girl slid on to the stool next to me and rocked it closer, whimpering softly but with little enthusiasm. I bought her a drink and went out. On the pavement a cat was rummaging in an empty paper bag.

Then I found Conchita, and together we drank *daiquiris* in the Habana Libre. She had lived for two years in Chicago, but now she wore *miliciana* uniform—with her jewellery—and spent her days trying to persuade small industrial workers to amalgamate and form co-operatives. It was uphill work. 'They are so conservative, they will not listen to me,' and she banged her bracelets on the butt of her revolver.

'I love Englishmen, your accent,' she said, moving closer. 'But Americans! When I see what the American papers say about Cuba,

177

when I know for myself it isn't true, I wonder how much of what they say about Russia is true.'

I was glad Conchita still wore her jewellery with her military shirt, her trousers and heavy boots. I was glad too that the *miliciano* who came to take her away had had his uniform made of special gabardine, and wore nylon socks and pointed Italian shoes. But I wasn't glad he came to take her away.

They left me with my *daiquiri*, and a feeling of mild desolation. It was those young men who worried me most; they fixed me with their blue eyes, clenched their fists, set their teeth, and before they had said a word my conscience was beginning to squirm. Were they trying to do too much, too quickly? Perhaps a short sharp shock was the best way, but their dedication was hardly less than fanaticism. However, they had a leader with the energy and the will to incite them to prodigious things, and even if it was muddled and inefficient they were doing it for themselves, not for the shareholders of some huge corporation. Cuba was on the move, and none of the other countries had begun.

I decided that it was only the cult I disliked, and the more-revolutionary-than-thou attitude; and I ordered another *daiquiri*. Suddenly I realized that everybody in the Habana Libre was on their feet, stock still; people had stopped like statues on the stairs, waiters were caught holding out trays, two women were standing back to back. There wasn't a smile or a word, but only the endless soft music streaming from the hidden loudspeakers. It must have been playing the national anthem.

There were some things I could never get used to. I could never learn to relax in a bus if the man next to me had his loaded pistol probing into my hip. I could never be quite happy going up in a lift alone with a delicious little *miliciana* of fifteen, a tommy-gun over her shoulder and her fingers idly fiddling with the trigger. Still less could I get used to the indignity of being frisked for weapons outside public buildings—standing with my arms in the air while a sentry sitting on a stool, a rifle across his knees and a cigar in his teeth, ran his hands up and down my body.

But the last time it happened, just before I left Havana, I was both angry enough and happy enough to tell the sentry that it was my birthday. He put down his gun and cigar, stood up and clutched my hand.

*   *   *

Geographically I had made a revolution, starting in Cuba and ending in Cuba. But emotionally too I had suffered another, more personal and more profound revolution. If I had not been to those other nine countries I should never have begun to understand the significance of what was happening in Cuba and what it meant to her neighbours. Revolution in another sense—not geographical but very much emotional, and political and economic as well—was blowing, in different ways, through all ten countries. It was in everybody's thoughts, on everybody's tongue, in everybody's heart.

Perhaps the hurricane that had hit Cuba would strike the others. If it did so it would bring the same trail of fury and disappointment, of destruction and subsequent construction that it brought to Cuba. During my last days in Havana I concerned myself with two aspects of the Cuban revolution that marked, I thought, the tragedy and the eventual benefit of that trail. The first was a film that lasted fifteen minutes and created an explosion that rumbled on for many months, demolishing the last hopes for liberty of many of the revolution's most fervid supporters. The second was Cuba's drastic, passionate answer to the biggest obstacle in the way of all backward, struggling countries—illiteracy.

*   *   *

The black shadow of an old motor launch slips across Havana harbour, blotting out the lights on the waterfront and stirring up the reflections. On board, twenty or thirty Cubans sit packed together on the wooden benches, in silence except for the pounding of the engine at their feet. The boat reaches the ferry pier, and before the gangway is put down most of the men have climbed over the gunwale and are heading for the gates. A woman passenger grins as she steps on to the jetty, and a man shouts something at her and laughs. They have come from one of the working-class suburbs across the harbour, beyond the big nationalized oil refineries, and they are going to make the most of a night out in Havana. He means to get drunk, and so probably does she.

The camera, following them all into the network of narrow streets behind the main dockyard road, enters a crowded bar and picks out a few chosen details: the barman pouring out white Bacardí rum, the figure of a drunk man wobbling happily to himself, the sweat on a negro's neck, the close-up of a huge female bottom. The Cuban bottom is inimitable; it strains and lunges with magnificent despair inside its skirt, but it is flared almost stylishly at the sides, like the stern of a cruiser; always, down the centre between the buttocks, a zip reaches to the thighs. This is a superb one, and the camera lingers on it.

During the next ten minutes the camera visits three more bars and shows Cubans, from the purest Spanish to the purest African with all the shades between, drinking, arguing, loving, quarrelling, dreaming. It falls on ecstasy and on desperation; it peers blearily through the cigar smoke, singles out a glass of beer, alights for a moment on a smile, winces at a bright electric bulb, hovers over a shelf of bottles. A blurred negress stands in front of the lens, and the camera moves back to take in the whole jostling, sweating scene.

In one of the bars there is a band playing, and the camera settles on a trumpeter's face, on the drums and on a pair of drumsticks clutched in a negro's hands, beating empty bottles. It moves to the revellers, scans their delirious faces, drops to their wiggling bodies and down to their jerking, staccato feet. The only sound is the roar of so many Cuban voices, the clink of glasses and ice from the bar, and the music. In the whole film there is not a single coherent word spoken.

Towards the end the revellers, exhausted with drinking and dancing, find themselves sitting in emptying bars, surrounded by deserted tables and watched impatiently by tired barmen. The impatience is infectious, and the drinkers themselves become peevish and quarrelsome. Women fling their arms about; men focus their eyes stickily on their glasses and wish they were already home. They
180

are exhausted, and only alcohol saves them from being more bad-tempered.

Finally the same old ferry-boat sounded its whistle and casts off from the jetty. Its shadow creeps back across the harbour in front of the waterfront lights, and the film flickers to an end.

Pasado Meridiano lasted just fifteen minutes, and I saw it surreptitiously in the corner of a blacked-out office high up in a Havana television building. It was made in January 1961 by two young Cubans; six months later it had become the centre of a first class rumpus among all the intellectuals of the country, and had been banned from public showing.

Saba Cabrera was twenty-eight, and Orlando Jiménez only nineteen when they made *Pasado Meridiano*. They shot it with an old sixteen-millimetre camera on film bought on the black market. They had no tripod or lights, but used only 'available light'; the sound was recorded at the same time on a small tape recorder. In all it cost them about a hundred pounds, and they received no help from anyone. It was their idea, achieved by their own enterprise and at their own expense, and they were more than just surprised to find that it landed them in the middle of a political storm.

When the film had been processed it was given a showing on a local television circuit, and with one exception was quite unnoticed by the critics. Only Nestor Almendros, film critic of *Bohemia*, the weekly magazine that, alone in Cuba, had pretentions at offering a serious and not too dogmatic comment on topical affairs, wrote a review of it. Almendros was a young Spaniard who left Franco's Spain and lived for some years in New York, where he made a remarkable film of the New Year's Eve celebration in Times Square. He went to Cuba after the Castro revolution, and became a Cuban citizen. He was the brother of the girl with the mesmerizing eyes in the Casa de las Americas.

In his review of *Pasado Meridiano* Almendros described it as 'a veritable jewel of experimental cinema', and 'enormously poetic'. It is understandable that he should have been enthusiastic about it, for as he said at the end it was exactly the kind of film which interested him most. 'Free cinema' was his own subject, and he welcomed any attempt by Cuban artists to create something that was both a spontaneous, unrehearsed account of the way some Cubans spend their nights, as well as a conscious artistic effort. From the film critic's personal point of view, too, it was refreshingly different from the average films he had to sit through, and he awarded it four stars, his highest mark. He could be excused for not mentioning that *Pasado Meridiano* was inclined to be amateurish, that much of the photography was not half as good as that of his own films, and that such comment as the film contained was little more than just reporting.

Cabrera and Jiménez were so encouraged by Almendros' review in *Bohemia* that they took their film to the manager of a small private cinema in Havana. He liked it, and said that he would show it in his programme, but that first they must get a licence from the Cuban Institute of Film Art and Industry, the state organization which controlled the import of all foreign films, the production of Cuban films and all cinema presentations, as well as the supply of all materials and equipment for making and processing films. They left their only copy of their film at the Institute and blithely expected that a licence would be just a formality. When they returned a few days later they were told that not only was any showing of the film prohibited, but that it was to be confiscated.

The storm broke immediately. Almendros, who had once worked for the Institute but had left it for television and criticism because he had found he was out of sympathy with the inflexible attitude of men whose ideas about making films were too different from his own, staunchly reiterated his original opinion of *Pasado Meridiano* and used his own influence to rally support for Cabrera and Jiménez. The Institute agreed to a private showing of the film at the Casa de las Americas, to which representatives of the ministries and all Cuba's intellectuals were invited.

After the film had been shown there was a discussion. Members of the Institute accused Cabrera and Jiménez of emphasizing counter-revolutionary attitudes in Cuban society and asked them what they had meant by this and that, and the two young men admitted that they hadn't really meant very much. But apart from
182

people connected directly with the government, almost the entire audience defended the film. At best, they argued, it was an original artistic expression, and at worst it was an amateurish documentary that was politically negative. And to prove that it did not depict a counter-revolutionary scene, somebody had gone down to the bars and clubs where it had been shot and interviewed people who appeared in it; every one of them was a revolutionary, and some of them were even *milicianos*.

Who, anyway, they asked, were the Institute men to talk? They themselves produced dreary socialist-realist stuff about *milicianos* and *alfabetizadores* that would convince nobody who was not already convinced. And worse still, they allowed the importation of terrible Hollywood trash, Westerns and British epics about battling on the North-west Frontier that portrayed imperialists as heroes and Indians as worse than animals—a far cry from the ideals of the Cuban revolution. Even some of the Russian and Polish films that were shown in Cuba were freer, more individualistic and sub-jective than *Pasado Meridiano*; only the Chinese films were as dreary as the Institute's—and as Almendros said, who wanted to make films like the Chinese?

The outraged intellectuals were led by the two editors—a novelist and a poet—of the culture supplement to the government news-paper, *Revolución*, which was published every Monday. To appease them the Institute suggested that the film should be shown to an unprejudiced audience for them to decide—the Trades Union Asso-ciation, or the Federation of Cuban Women. But that annoyed the intellectuals even more. What did trade unionists or women know about films? It was obvious that either organization would produce the verdict they knew was expected of them. Instead, they asked for a vote to be taken there and then; to which the Institute replied that voting was a revisionist practice and had no place in the Cuban revolution. As a concession they handed *Pasado Meridiano* back to Cabrera and Jiménez, on condition that it was never to be shown.

The intellectuals then signed a manifesto and sent it to Castro, and a few days later it was announced that the forthcoming Con-gress of Cuban Writers and Artists, to which people from all the socialist countries had been invited, was postponed—because Havana airport was to be closed down for an extension of the runway. Another big meeting was held, this time with Castro and President Dorticós, members of ministries, newspapers and the Film Institute and about eighty intellectuals. The intellectuals accused the government of Stalinism, of destroying the spirit of the revolution and of dangerously antagonizing Cuban artists. Culture was in the hands of two or three elderly women and a handful of diehards, and the younger generation was smothered. Thenceforth unless it was saved and nurtured into something new, Cuban and revolutionary, it would plunge through a welter of bureaucracy into a black abyss of dogma, for which the Cuban people had no taste. *Pasado Meridiano*, a trifle that was of no consequence in itself, had become a symbol.

' If the intellectuals only wanted a show-down,' said an Englishman, ' they should have waited for something a little better than *Pasado Meridiano*. It's a dud.' But the intellectuals were in a hurry.

A few days later I met Almendros by a swimming-pool with Cabrera, who was in *miliciano* uniform. Almendros had just been sacked from his job as film critic of *Bohemia*. He hadn't been summoned by the editor, but had been told the news by the man who had been appointed to succeed him. The bitterest blow, however, had come from another film critic, a man who was a notorious opportunist and who had been concerned with a dreadful film about José Martí in the days of Batista. At the private showing of *Pasado Meridiano* in the Casa de las Americas he had been one of the loudest to clap, but later he had suddenly changed his mind. When Almendros asked him why, he replied that he had only applauded the technique of the film, but that the content was bad. He then turned on Almendros and accused him of defending counter-revolutionary films. And then he accused him of being a Fascist.

' Me, a Fascist ! ' cried Almendros. ' A pacifist, yes; but a Fascist ! I left Franco's Spain because it was Fascist, I came here to work for the revolution, I became a Cuban citizen. Me, a Fascist ! '

An actress, a pretty, foolish girl, was sitting in a deck-chair by the pool. Almendros called her over and asked her if she

thought it was right that he should be sacked from *Bohemia*.
' Well,' she said, ' I don't know all the facts, you see.'

That was typical, said Almendros, of the young. They had no opinions now and they didn't want to argue. Later, he was sure, she would go off and tell her friends how good it was that *Bohemia* was rid of him, a Fascist like that.

But he wasn't really bitter. He would go on working for the revolution as long as he could. The only trouble was that there were no intellectuals among the leaders. None of them ever read any books or listened to music. They simply didn't have time. They were all too busy running the revolution.

Some months later the Monday culture supplement of *Revolución* was suddenly closed down by the government, and the staff disbanded; the senior editor was offered the job of Cuban ambassador to North Korea. About the same time I received a postcard from Almendros, from Czechoslovakia. He sounded happy.

*   *   *

Alfabetización is a very long word, but in Cuba in 1961 it was being bandied about with marvellous fluency by *alfabetizados*, *alfabetizadores*, and even by mere *analfabetos*. The year 1961 was officially christened at its birth the Year of Education, just as 1959 had been the Year of Revolution and 1960 the Year of Agrarian Reform; all the problems of educating a backward population were being tackled with terrific energy, but the chief object of 1961 was the huge task of ridding Cuba of illiteracy. At the beginning of the year thirty per cent of the population—about two million people— couldn't read or write, and to teach them all needed a campaign of pretty big proportions, particularly as most of the illiterates were peasants living in the countryside or up in the mountains, far from any school.

Such was the dauntlessness of Cuba's leaders that the acute shortage of teachers, though Cuba had doubled the number in two years, was no obstacle; with seven million people living on the island, of whom five million could read and write and two million couldn't, it was obvious where to look for people to teach the illiterates.

About a quarter of a million men and women, known as *alfabetizadores populares*, volunteered to conduct private literacy classes in their spare time, for no wages. These formed the majority of the teachers in the campaign, but because they were workers themselves, or housewives, they could only give up two or three hours a day to teaching, and they could not leave the town or village where they lived to teach people in remoter districts. The job of carrying the battle into the backwoods of illiteracy, where hundreds of thousands of peasants were still languishing in ignorance, as unable to read the revolutionary newspapers and pamphlets as their own cattle, was given to a section of society which could be relied on to campaign with enthusiasm and even high spirits—Cuba's schoolchildren. And as well as bringing the blessings of literacy to the peasants, the children too would benefit; for such an important, spectacular task would give them a sense of being actively involved in the revolution, and thus make them, if not heroes, at least better revolutionaries.

At the beginning of April all the state schools broke up for the holidays (all private schools, which meant catholic ones, were closed at the same time and never re-opened) and the children were told that they would not be expected back until November; the whole of the summer term was to be missed out, and instead the children were to go off into the countryside and teach the alphabet to anyone, of any age, who was unlucky enough not to know it.

To the prospect of a six-month summer holiday as a *brigadista* was added the irresistible attraction of taking over their own teacher's job, and little propaganda was needed to induce the children to enrol, though they had to have their parents' consent; by the end of the campaign it was expected that eighty per cent of all secondary school children between twelve and eighteen years old, with a sprinkling of younger children down to only nine, would have become *brigadistas*. And at the end of the year, at a rally in Havana to celebrate the *brigadistas'* return from the countryside, it was going to be announced that illiteracy had been banished from the land.

186

About eighty miles east of Havana is a seaside resort called Varadero, with one of the finest white sand beaches in the Caribbean. American tourists used to fly there direct from Florida, and there are several luxury hotels, as well as many seaside villas owned by rich Cubans. But nowadays there are no tourists, and most of the rich Cubans have taken themselves off, with their riches if they are lucky, to Miami. Varadero has become a state holiday resort, with huge new blocks of flats for holidaying workers and peasants; the beach, which was once the preserve of the plutocrats and the foreign tourists, has been opened to the people. But in 1961 Varadero had become more than just a socialist Blackpool. It was the place where the *brigadistas* were given their brief training, and fitted out with uniform and weapons for their campaign.

It all began in the middle of April, when a special branch of the National Commission of Alphabetization, a department of the Ministry of Education, was opened in the former Yacht Club at Varadero, and buses of school-children from all provinces of Cuba began to arrive. When I went to Varadero at the end of June there were a hundred teachers and two hundred physical training instructors there; 55,000 children had already passed through a one-week course and been sent out to teach. By July 26th, the anniversary date of Castro's revolutionary movement, when training courses were due to end, nearly a hundred thousand boys and girls—with a small majority of girls—were expected to have passed through. Varadero was then to close down, and the job left to the *brigadistas*.

The scene in the Yacht Club was typical of all executive departments in revolutionary Cuba. In the small office overlooking the yacht basin a young man in grey uniform, the director, was sitting at a desk talking into a telephone and at the same time trying to answer the questions of a persistent young woman opposite him. In other corners were more young men and women, sitting on the furniture or the floor, thumping typewriters, telephoning and talking in the noisy Cuban way. Everywhere lay cigar butts, empty Coca-Cola bottles, coffee cups and revolver holsters. The atmosphere was a mixture of frenzy and dedication, laced with cigar smoke.

Outside, beyond the terrace and green lawns of the Yacht Club,

187

was the yacht basin, with several hundred small boys of all colours in swimming trunks lining up for trips on two magnificent Bermudan yachts. The sight of those yachts drifting up and down the inland basin under their engines, with their decks invisible beneath a mass of almost naked boys, might have surprised their ex-owners, wherever they were. All the other yachts moored to the jetty lay idle, slowly bleaching in the Caribbean sun.

The excitement for the children, most of whom had never before seen a smart holiday resort, let alone been allowed to use its facilities, must have been overwhelming. It was emphatically and deliberately a week's holiday, but the children also spent three hours a day being instructed on their job of teaching the alphabet, on simple first aid and hygiene and on revolutionary doctrine. The boys were lodged in the new flats, which had not yet been used by the workers and peasants for whom they were built, and the girls in the rich men's villas just behind the beach.

One particularly hideous villa, a vulgar sprawl of brown and blue concrete, had a plaque in the porch saying that it had won the Cuban Architecture Prize in 1946. Inside, on the walls, were huge cement bas-reliefs, turquoise and pink, of nudes and sailing ships, and execrable portraits of some millionaire's family; there was even a private bowling-alley, and the ugliest staircase I have ever seen, winding up to the bedrooms. But now the house had been expropriated, and there were nearly two hundred girls living in it, sleeping in double bunks crammed into every room; the whole house was filled with girlish shrieks. In one room a beauty salon had been set up, where a negro girl was having her hair shampooed and others were learning to wave and set, so that they could teach the peasant women.

Any children who couldn't swim were given lessons, all of them were X-rayed for tuberculosis, and for most of their week at Varadero they played games, swam or went for boat trips. But even in that socialist institution there were traces of old-fashioned superstition; on the path down to the beach was a notice cautioning the children not to bathe within three hours after a meal. And on the beach there were life-savers sitting up on high chairs, like tennis

188

umpires, shouting at the children through megaphones if they strayed too far in the surf.

Watching bus loads of excited children arriving with their parcels and suitcases from all over Cuba and being detailed off to their accommodation, I was reminded of a new intake of recruits joining the army—but with an optimism and exuberance unknown in any barracks. And watching bus loads of *brigadistas* in new uniform, with their green knapsacks on their backs and hurricane lamps clutched in their hands, setting off to spread the words throughout the land, I was moved by the determination of a country to tackle the most serious obstacle to the development of all backward peoples, by the inspiration of its leaders at thinking of such an effective and swift method, and by the energy of its children.

After their week's training at Varadero the children joined the army of *alfabetizadores*, with thirty *brigadistas* in each platoon, a hundred in a company, five hundred in a battalion and two thousand in a brigade. In the army, as at Varadero, the boys and girls were strictly segregated, and in theory at least the girls were sent to the villages and the settlements centred round sugar mills, and the boys to the more isolated districts.

The commander of each unit, from brigade down to platoon, was an executive officer in charge of the movements of his troops, financing them and directing their movements, but he had one qualified teacher on his staff, to give technical advice. On the average, each *brigadista* had between seven and ten illiterate peasants to teach, and the whole summer to do it in.

On arriving at his post the young *brigadista* made a census of the district, plotting every illiterate peasant and enrolling his name in the register of *analfabetos*. As soon as possible he got down to work, teaching the women by day and the men when they came home from work at night. He was expected also to help the peasants in their work, partly in order to make himself useful and help pay for his food, and partly to achieve better relations with them and break down any resentment they might have at being educated. With his platoon commander he signed the certificate given to every peasant on achieving literacy, and with his pupil he signed a letter

189

which the triumphant peasant wrote to Fidel Castro, asking for a book as a token of his success.

He was also obliged to read his manual every day, and to contribute, by his own example, to improving the sanitary habits of the peasants among whom he lived. He had to show respect to the people he was lodged with, and if possible give them a share of the ten dollars a month he received as pocket money; he had to keep a diary in which to put down everything of interest that he noticed, as well as his own experiences; he had to write home to his family regularly; and he was responsible for looking after his uniform and his equipment.

This equipment, the *brigadista's* armoury, was issued to him at the end of his week at Varadero. It consisted of a paraffin hurricane lamp, a magnificent chromium machine made in the People's Republic of China and costing, as every visitor was tediously told, only a quarter of the price of a similar lamp made in the United States. And he was given a knapsack containing a hammock, four pencils, notebooks, copies of five of Castro's speeches on education, a reader called *Venceremos* (' We shall conquer ') for his pupils and a manual called *Alfabeticemos* (' We are alphabetizing ') for himself, a pamphlet called *Arma Nueva* containing articles on subjects ranging from the United States naval base at Guantánamo to the iniquities of European imperialism in Africa, blank certificates of the elementary, intermediate and final grades of literacy, various other pamphlets about how to teach reading and writing and arithmetic, how to show the peasants ways of reducing their own plight and of working more efficiently for the revolution, how to operate the hurricane lamp, how to prevent water pollution, how and where to dig a well, how to build an earth closet, how to persuade the peasants to wash their fruit and vegetables and hands and feet and teeth and bodies and clothes, to keep their food clean, to boil their milk and to keep their farm animals out of their houses. Also in the knapsack, in case such a load should be too daunting for such youthful teachers, was a tin of condensed milk, a couple of bars of chocolate, and a bag of boiled sweets.

The leaders of the National Commission of Alphabetization made
190

no bones about the fact that the campaign was political as well as pedagogic. The *brigadista's* first duty was to teach, but he was reminded that he would be considered a strange and novel person by the peasants among whom he lived, that he would be watched with suspicion, that any clumsy interference on his part would be resented and that his conduct had to be exemplary. The Cuban peasants, he was told, were a noble people who had been treated all too abominably by feudalism and imperialism, but for whom enlightenment would bring prosperity; he therefore had to do all he could, by living as a member of a peasant family and by helping with his hosts' work, to win their respect and confidence, and then lose no opportunity of teaching them about the revolution.

As soon as he started to learn the alphabet, a Cuban peasant was plunged instantly into politics. The first lesson in *Venceremos*, the pupil's reader, consisted of the three vowels, O, E and A, which are the initials of the Organization of American States, and the accompanying chapter in *Alfabeticemos*, the teachers' manual, was a disquisition on foreign affairs covering the fate of all other countries in Latin America beneath the oppression of Yankee imperialism, the significance for the whole continent of the Cuban revolution, and even touching on the usurpation by the puppet government in Formosa of China's rightful seat in the United Nations.

It might seem a little ambitious to expect an illiterate peasant, shakily tracing his first three vowels, to have to grapple with the implications of world politics as well, but the next few lessons brought him nearer home; they dealt with the benefits of agrarian reform, farming and fishery co-operatives and the militia. As the peasant pupils spelt out the sentences from his reader—'we are masters of our wealth', 'the Cuban of today is free', 'there will be houses for everyone'—his child teacher read out the appropriate chapter in the manual. Some of it was more innocent—'Gilbert is an engineer', and 'Cecilia reads the news'—but the peasant struggling with his alphabet also learnt about the nature of true democracy, the cruelties of capitalism and the glory of the Cuban revolution under the guidance of its *Máximo Líder*.

At the end of the manual was a short vocabulary of words which might possibly have puzzled the pupils and which his master could explain for him. Thus 'Associated Press', for example, was a North American news agency in the service of Yankee imperialism; 'economic blockade' was the state of siege which imperialism had imposed on the Cuban revolution; 'collective revolutionary vigilance' was an organization of the popular masses devoted to attacking the action of counter-revolutionary elements by means of universal participation; and 'sub-soil' was simply what lies below the soil.

But it is too easy to make fun of the more absurd, or more sinister, aspects of the campaign, and to forget its real significance. Education is the crying need for all under-developed countries, and Cuba was tackling the problem with an energy unequalled in Latin America. It is tempting to be cynical, to argue that the Cuban leaders were only interested in literacy so that their subjects could be more easily indoctrinated, and even to doubt if a hundred thousand schoolchildren let loose in the Cuban countryside for a few months could really have much effect. But what is certain is that for the first time the Cuban peasants were being made aware of their own ignorance, and being provoked into doing something about it.

In the centre of Varadero, a few yards from the beach and among all the requisitioned villas, was a new modern block, partly underground, that obviously belonged to Varadero the state holiday camp rather than Varadero the ex-resort. It was an enormous circular cafeteria, where waitresses dispensed fizzy drinks with the disgruntled charmlessness common to all such places. Radiating round the cafeteria were rows of changing cubicles, showers, lockers, washrooms and lavatories. There was a locker with a key for every bather. My Cuban guide, demonstrating the amenities, pushed open the door of a lavatory. The bowl was clogged, and he hastily pulled the plug, apologizing for the absent-mindedness of some unknown compatriot. We tried the next lavatory, but that too was clogged.

'Education,' said the Cuban, sadly pulling the second plug. 'That's the first thing—education.'